WHEN EVIL REIGNS

THE TIMELINE OF THE ANTICHRIST'S
IMMINENT RISE TO POWER

WHEN EVIL REIGNS

JOHN AND KATHERINE FORD

TATE PUBLISHING & *Enterprises*

Published by Tate Publishing & Enterprises, LLC
127 E. Trade Center Terrace | Mustang, Oklahoma 73064 USA
1.888.361.9473 | www.tatepublishing.com

Tate Publishing is committed to excellence in the publishing industry. The company reflects the philosophy established by the founders, based on Psalm 68:11,
"The Lord gave the word and great was the company of those who published it."

Book design copyright © 2010 by Tate Publishing, LLC. All rights reserved.
Cover design by Amber Gulilat
Interior design by Jeff Fisher

Published in the United States of America

ISBN: 978-1-61663-661-6
1. Religion, Christian Theology, Eschatology
2. Religion, Biblical Studies, Prophecy
10.08.17

ACKNOWLEDGED TO BE ONE OF HISTORY'S
WISEST MEN, SOLOMON STATES:

*"THE THING THAT HAS BEEN—IT IS WHAT WILL
BE AGAIN, AND THAT WHICH HAS BEEN DONE IS
THAT WHICH WILL BE DONE AGAIN; AND THERE IS
NOTHING NEW UNDER THE SUN."*

(ECCLESIASTES 1:9, TAB)

DEDICATION

To Steven, our son and friend, we have chosen to dedicate this book to you for two simple reasons: One is to tell you how much we love you and appreciate that you are always there for us, and second, but most importantly, this book is about the future—God's future and your future. Heaven would not be heaven without you!

TABLE OF CONTENTS

INTRODUCTION

Technology, information, and knowledge in general are advancing at a record pace. The world has gotten smaller as computers and satellites have allowed us to reach into the far recesses of the earth with a few swipes of the keyboard. It is a scenario quite conducive for globalization—One-World Government, One-World Religion, and the cashless society into which we are plunging headlong. These not-so-new ideas are being put forth by some very influential people and groups. The European Union and United Nations are great proponents of these forward-thinking measures. The UN is more than a proponent, and one might even say a puppet, of the New Age Movement, which will give you a hint of the new, singular world religion.

While our physical world seems to be rushing forward toward the New World Order everyone has been talking about, things have also been accelerated in the spiritual world. Everything we are going through has been prophecied as being part of the end times, setting up a world that is perfect for the son of Satan—the antichrist—to rule over. There is a plan that has been in place since the beginning of time, and that plan is about to be manifested. This also means that the end of the world is near, but first, Satan must find his ideal candidate, the personification of evil, to do his bidding.

God has used types and shadows throughout the Old Testament to point the way to Jesus. Well Satan—being the copier he is—has done something similar. He has people who have been precursors of the coming antichrist. By Satan's standards, and by comparison to the coming Son of Perdition, these have been minor players in the past—call them trial run antichrists, such as Charlemagne, Otto I, Bismarck, and of course, Adolf Hitler, with Hitler being the most recent and perhaps most successful. Building upon this success, and perhaps even using Hitler as a model, the devil is about to reveal his shining star.

Through many hours of research and deductive reasoning, some of the answers this world has been searching for concerning the antichrist and his rise to power will be revealed. There is an amazing parallel between the life and times of Hitler and the coming antichrist. There is also a time frame that depicts this parallel and helps us to set up a scenario that is both naturally possible and spiritually accurate. In other words, some of the missing end-times pieces based on logic and historic events will be filled in.

Even though it may be somewhat controversial, this book was written because it projects a probable scenario of the days ahead. All available resources have been used to help make our case. It is presented not because there is anything anyone can do to change it, but because knowledge is power. If this book serves to turn around one life, then it will be worth its writing. It is a warning that there are choices to be made—choices that should not be put off. The days of heaven and hell clashing are imminent; which side will you be on?

CHAPTER ONE:

THE FUTURE IN WHICH WE LIVE

THE FUTURE IS NOW,
THOUGH WRIT YESTERDAY.

IT ALL COMES TOGETHER
AS GOD HAS HIS SAY.

What if I were to tell you that the antichrist is alive today? It is a startling revelation, for sure, but all the speculation is true—we are living in the end times. I can't help but smile as I read the first two sentences of this book. They take me back several decades, when as a young person stopped at a red light, I noticed a homeless-looking man on the median strip of the road. He was unshaven and clearly needed a bath. A worn sandwich board sign hung from his bony shoulders. I could see, "Repent!" written boldly on the front of the sign. My curiosity aroused, I inched my car forward to get a glimpse of the back. On the back, scrawled in big red letters, the sign read, "The end is near!"

Coming back to reality, I sit with fingers poised on the keyboard and can't help but chuckle to myself. I wonder if this is the picture my readers will get as they read those first two sentences, but let me assure you that while these may seem like inflammatory statements, they are ones that will be played out within the pages of this book. It will be proven through history, prophecy, and archaeology, as well as through current international politics, that what is written here is not only possible but even probable. This is the last generation, and it is either blessed or cursed, depending which side you are on.

A POLARIZED NATION

The world is getting smaller every day. Technological advances are happening faster than we can learn about them. Our current events are forward-moving, prophecy-fulfilling whirlwinds that seem to be on a collision course with eternity. The schism between nations, religions, races, and even families grows wider every day. What seemed like a world with plenty of room for gray has turned very black and white. The line between good and evil and right and wrong has been smudged, yet it has never been clearer. There are choices to be made—important choices.

It's like the earth itself has shifted, and many things we Americans thought were forever have shifted too. We are not the super power we once were. We have lost the respect of other nations and have taken a backseat to many who, just decades ago, would have been considered primitive. Our government is corrupt and failing.

The bad news is that we are a nation split right down the middle on most major issues. A battle of cultures and ideologies has polarized this country. The unity that once was ours is forever lost in a sea of selfishness and indifference. Have you noticed how today's patriotism is held up by the older generation? Have you seen how eroded our principles, morals, and even our lifestyles have become? Have you recognized how anxious we are to join the world in complete compromise and unprecedented tolerance?

Our world has been turned upside down. We have raised a generation of Americans who do not believe in absolute truth. The very ideology that we were once shouting to the universe has gone out of fashion. We can only whisper the truth in corners. Why? Because we are told there cannot be only one truth. Truth is relative, they say, and everyone in this world has a right to their own truth. This thinking has eroded our morals, denigrated our forefathers, and lied to our children.

TOLERANCE

There is one secular commandment today that the world seems to follow: Above all else, we must be *tolerant!* This is the new god of the world—the thing we worship most, but we can no longer be selective in our tolerance. *All* must be tolerated! We must tolerate that which offends us and most of the citizenry of our nation. We must condone that which in our hearts we know is wrong. We must embrace people and policies that clearly represent evil.

Why? Because it appeals to our basest nature, because it makes anything we do right, and because it gives us permissions to make the rules or ignore them. We can do and be and think whatever suits our fancy. It assuages all guilt, and it brings us closer to what we already suspect—that we know best, we are all in charge of ourselves, and we are the little gods who rule our own lives and tolerate others who do the same. Isn't that generous of us?

However, the worst part of this new pluralism is that you cannot just be tolerant of another's beliefs or ideas. At one time, being tolerant simply meant making room for someone else's point of view but not necessarily agreeing with them. Now you cannot express an opinion; you cannot say you think someone is wrong or even intimate it. You must even tolerate those who directly attack your God. Not to do so automatically labels you as intolerant, prejudiced, and narrow-minded.

ALLOWING A PLACE

Tolerance for others' actions or beliefs is one thing; it should simply mean you allow a place for it. They may believe or do as they please. To infer that tolerance has to do with a full acceptance of another's ideas, however—whether or not you think they are wrong—is just ridiculous. First of all, there can be only one truth, so if you are convinced that you know the truth, how can accepting someone else's truth be right or beneficial? What we have done, in effect, with pluralism is say we must tolerate everything whether or not it is true, logical, or even rational.

This goes well with the no absolutes, situational ethics, and behavior modification mind-sets, all of which are fundamental New Age principles. When everyone has their own truth, then tolerance becomes a non-issue, and everything is tolerated as long as one person believes it.

In the midst of all this limitless tolerance, there is one thing we must not tolerate, and that is God. He is the enemy. He is the one who represents standards to a world that wants to identify and live by its own rules. Therefore, God cannot represent absolute truth and, therefore, must not be tolerated. However, the real question then becomes: "How long will God tolerate us?"

HISTORICAL ROOTS

The irony is overpowering when you consider that all of our nation's historical documents strove, first and foremost, to promote tolerance of religion. That was their purpose for the founding of this country. It was the basis for the American Revolution. Tolerance, then, meant freedom to worship as one pleased. The authors of the Declaration of Independence and the Constitution, our forefathers, began a new nation. Almost all of them were Christian in belief, though of differing sects, and they guaranteed that same tolerance that now wants to exclude its authors—its founders. Was this the same kind of tolerance we are talking about today? No, it wasn't.

At that time, there were no adverse beliefs to the Christian faith that were part of this tolerance. When our forefathers spoke of tolerance, they were speaking of an acceptance and inclusion of all *Christian* sects. This tolerance did not extend to believing or even necessarily welcoming other faiths. Having mostly come from England, where there was one official church, and therefore one state-sanctioned belief, there was little room for other denominations.

The type of tolerance they were hoping to instill in this new nation was Christian. It doesn't seem likely that our founders made a place for immorality and non-Christian behavior and beliefs when they wrote and voted on the First Amendment. The strange thing is that we have become very open and accepting of other, totally different religions—those with very different morals and mores—that are themselves intolerant of Christianity and our Judeo-Christian heritage.

Today, being intolerant of the principles and truths that structured this great land of ours just shows how far we've come and how much we've lost. We no longer believe we need a Creator to look up to; we are smart enough to make our own decisions. Most are not aware of it, but this new brand of tolerance that says individuals set the standard is exactly what has turned this world upside down.

WE ARE LIVING PROPHECY

Whether or not you are "religious," or even if you doubt the existence of God, upon proper study, one must admit that one book—the Bible, which was written centuries ago by many hands—is remarkably and miraculously accurate. The statements that were made hundreds or thousands of years ago that seemed impossible have found a way—oddly enough, through the choices we've made—to manifest themselves. It's quite comforting for Christians to watch historical predictions coming true right before their eyes, thus proving once and for all that there is a greater truth—an absolute truth.

For almost 2,000 years now, we have listened to doomsday prophets and fanatical ramblings about the end of the world. These strange prognosticators have unwittingly set the stage for the diabolical plot that has been unleashed in this generation, only now it is backed by truth. History, archeological finds, Biblical prophecy, and international politics put us at the crossroads of World War III and certain mass destruction. Add to this the volatile religious world situation—including radical Islam and anti-Semitism—and many of these so-called weirdos of yesteryear seem like real prophets with a timing problem.

The purpose of this book is not to set the date of Christ's second coming, but there are some new insights to share. You will find this to be more than a little interesting—perhaps even intriguing. While this book is not just about fulfilled prophecy, we will begin there.

First of all, the Bible has many secrets yet to be revealed. If you are interested in this topic, you might be amazed at some of the prophecies that are written in the Bible regarding end times—prophecies that have already been fulfilled. This book will point out a few of these, perform a few logical analyses, and come up with some real possibilities for these last days that make sense to all.

A MOST ACCURATE TOME

Over the centuries, the Bible has come under tremendous scrutiny by those who want to either prove or disprove its accuracy. In fact, it's reasonable to state that no other document has undergone as much critical evaluation, yet no one has ever disproved its accuracy—actually, quite the opposite. Many of those who started out to discredit the Bible have found the Bible's incredible validity and have become among its staunchest supporters. Prominent people such as C.S. Lewis (*Mere Christianity*), Lee Strobel (*The Case For Christ*), and Lew Wallace (*Ben Hur, A Tale of Christ*) are just a few who once considered themselves to be atheist, agnostic, or "indifferent to religion." Their lives were literally turned around in their quest to prove there was no God.

There are those who think that because the Bible is an ancient book, written by many authors, it has numerous inaccuracies and inconsistencies. That's not true. Modern archeology has played an important role in confirming Bible accuracy. We now possess more than 5,300 known Greek manuscripts of the New Testament. Add over 10,000 Latin Vulgate and at least 9,300 other early versions, and we have more than 24,000 manuscript copies of portions of the New Testament in existence, starting from the second century.

All of these manuscripts tell the same story and are quite consistent with each other. No other document of this age approaches such numbers. Of course, we also have the more ancient Dead Sea Scrolls, from about 100 BC, which precisely mirror the Old Testament as it is written today.

A frequent misconception is that a close study of the Bible will prove that only faith, not fact, supports this religion. Actually, a careful study of Bible prophecy has converted many, including atheists, because the manifestation of the predictions totally and accurately fulfilled is so compelling that it leaves no room for discussion or denial. When all is said and done, you will learn that the accuracy rate of the Bible's fulfilled predictions is frighteningly correct—almost one hundred percent. For example, only one prediction in the Old Testament concerning Christ's life, death, and resurrection is not confirmed elsewhere, and that involved Roman soldiers plucking the hair of Jesus' beard as they tortured Him. However, this certainly seems a likely possibility.

FORETOLD

Both the Old and New Testaments are peppered with prophecy, which is simply foretelling what will happen in the future. There's probably no more controversial subject in the Bible, yet about thirty percent of the Bible concerns prophecy. Because it is difficult to understand and often symbolic in nature, and because it deals with the future and spiritual matters, even many staunch Christians avoid the subject. That, however, is a mistake, since it is a most effective tool in disproving many fallacies concerning Christianity.

There are over three hundred prophecies in the Old Testament concerning the first coming of the Messiah. When repetitions are eliminated, we're left with 108 different prophecies, all but one of which were verified as fulfilled during the life and death of Jesus Christ on Earth. The odds of fulfilling so many prophecies are statistically overwhelming. Using the method of Professor Emeritus of Science Peter Stoner at Westmont College, the statistical odds of fulfilling so many prophecies occurring coincidentally amounts to 1 in 10 to the 157th power or a 10 followed by 157 zeros (Stoner 2003, 1).

While some could be affected by a person's own actions, others, like place of birth, would be beyond His control. Please note that the Jews, who hold the Old Testament sacred, do not deny that these prophecies are in the Old Testament or that they were at least partially fulfilled in the life and death of Jesus. Their major point of dispute is that they didn't believe He was the Messiah.

Of course, the Old Testament is not the only place where we find fulfilled prophecy. For example, around AD 30, His disciples point out to Jesus what an imposing structure the Jewish temple in Jerusalem was. Jesus said that it would be destroyed, and "…not one stone shall be left here upon another…" (Matthew 24:2).

NEW TESTAMENT PROPHECIES

About forty years later, the Roman soldiers burned the temple. They realized, as they watched the burning structure, that they had left some gold inside, because as the temperature rose, the gold was liquefied and began to seep into the cracks between the stones. When the stone cooled, they took pry bars to the structure and examined each stone individually for a residue of gold, thus fulfilling the prophecy—leaving no stone "...that shall not be thrown down."

Jesus also foretold of the fall of three cities in Galilee: Capernaum, Chorazin, and Bethsaida (Matthew 11:21–24). The fifth and tenth Roman legions began a systematic devastation of the country in 65 AD. These three cities were decimated, and the remaining residents were enslaved. Earthquakes finished the job. These cities exist no more, yet others nearby, such as Tiberias, stand to this day.

It is not difficult to look back on events and see how they were foretold, but it is much harder to believe in things yet to come. Of course, with the passage of time, we can see the future more clearly. We do know through technology today that many things that would have seemed impossible just several decades ago are now clearly possible, if not probable. From a practical point of view, the rise of radical Islam and the proliferation of weapons of mass destruction makes some of the scenes in the Book of Revelation seem much more likely. You may think that this is overstating the facts, but before deciding, take a walk through some rather recent events, historically speaking.

THE DISPERSION OF THE JEWS IN PROPHECY

In centuries gone by, it would have been unfathomable to see Israel as an independent nation. The dispersion of the Jews was already a fulfilled prophecy. No one could argue that the Jewish people, who were once a nation, were scattered throughout the world, just as predicted.

"Then they shall know that I am the Lord, when I scatter them among the nations and disperse them throughout the countries" (Ezekiel 12:15).

Luke 21:24 says, "And they will fall by the edge of the sword, and be led away captive into all nations. And Jerusalem will be trampled by Gentiles until the times of the Gentiles are fulfilled."

Biblical prophecy scholars agree that the end times could not occur without the reemergence of the state of Israel, but for many hundreds of years, there seemed little likelihood of that occurring. Thus, prophets of the end times, without explanation, tended to just ignore this obvious fact. In retrospect, however, we know that all of the prophecies relating to the Jews being dispersed and then re-gathered have been fulfilled.

> Then the Lord will scatter you among all peoples, from one end of the earth to the other and there you shall serve other gods, which neither you nor your fathers have known-wood and stone. And among those nations you shall find no rest, nor shall the sole of your foot have a resting place; but there the Lord will give you a trembling heart, failing eyes, and anguish of soul. Your life shall hang in doubt before you; you shall fear day and night, and have no assurance of life. In the morning you shall say, "Oh, that it were evening!" and at evening you shall say, "Oh, that it were morning!" because of the fear which terrifies your heart, and because of the sight which your eyes see.
>
> Deuteronomy 28:64–67

JEWISH PERSECUTION

These scriptures and many others left no doubt that Jews were to be a people disjointed, living in pockets of persecution throughout the world. History has borne witness to this. It was

AD 70 when the Romans destroyed Jerusalem and killed over one million Jews. By AD 200, the Jews were forbidden to read the Torah or practice circumcision, and conversion to Judaism was outlawed. It was AD 306 when marriages were banned and all community contacts were forbidden between Christians and Jews. Between AD 379 and 395, Christianity became the state religion of the Roman Empire, and all synagogues that served a religious purpose were destroyed.

In the year 528, Emperor Justinian, ruler of the eastern Roman Empire, passed the Justinian code, which prohibited Jews from reading the Bible in Hebrew or assembling in public. It also contained many other restrictions, including a ban on testifying against Christians in court. By 612, Jews were not allowed to own land or enter certain trades, including farming.

Jewish persecution actually gained momentum, and between 1096 and 1099, the first Crusade began. All the Jews of Jerusalem were forced into a synagogue, and the synagogue was set on fire. Between 1290 and 1354, Jews were exiled from England, Austria, Bavaria, Franconia, and Toledo.

ANTI-SEMITISM GOES WAY BACK

In 1492, the year Columbus discovered America, the Jews were given an ultimatum: Be baptized as Christians, or be banished from Spain. Portugal followed suit five years later. Martin Luther, after failing to convert the Jews, turned against them and preached hatred in 1523. In 1550, Jews were banished from Genoa and Venice. In 1582, they were exiled from Holland. More than 100,000 Jews were killed and 300 communities destroyed in an uprising against Polish rule in the Ukraine in 1648 and 1649.

From about 1800, anti-Semitism became a form of racism. Rumors flew, and governments used any excuse to ban, terrorize, or kill Jews; this attitude was pervasive through the nineteenth century. In 1881, when Alexander II was murdered, the Jews were blamed. In the early twentieth century, Russian Jews became a target, and hundreds of thousands of them were killed by starvation or outright slaughter. Two hundred thousand Jews were murdered in the Ukraine alone following the Bolshevik Revolution of 1917.

Despite all this, no time in history—no persecution—can compare to the years of torture and slaughter that the targeted Jews endured at the hands of one madman and a country of mostly good Christian people, thoroughly deceived.

THE HOLOCAUST

Imagine waking up on any ordinary day, kissing your husband good-bye, and getting your baby up and dressed. Now, imagine the year is 1942, and you are a Jew in Nazi Germany. You live in a ghetto—a small, walled-in Jewish community where you have to be careful of your every move. A wrong glance or word could get you robbed or beaten. It doesn't matter if you walk straight ahead with your eyes on the pavement; you may still be singled out for some persecution as a joke for the Nazis.

Each time you leave your home, you just pray to be invisible and that you make it back in one piece with your groceries. Your husband, a banker by trade, is coerced into forced labor with meager wages, but you reason that at least you are all together. Every evening, you breathe a sigh of relief as you sit down to the sparse offerings before you to give thanks for another day of life.

The days go into weeks, and the weeks drag into months, and each and every day you hear rumors and tales of horror and wonder if life will ever be right again. There are sounds of distant gunfire and screams that reverberate in the air. One day, you hear the goose-step marching of the SS. As the sound grows closer, you take your four-month-old baby, put tape over his mouth, and put him in a suitcase already prepared with a blanket and breathing holes.

HERDED LIKE CATTLE

There's a pounding on your door and before you can get out any words, they have forced their way into your apartment. You are rounded up with the rest of your neighbors, told nothing, and herded like cattle into an already overcrowded railroad boxcar. You ride for what seems an eternity, and with no windows, the stench of human bodies huddled together to keep out the cold is almost too much to bear. Your thoughts wander to your husband; you pray that he escaped this awful fate.

When you disembark, you are prodded to gather on the ramp, at which time you are divided into two groups. You are directed to the left, which you later find out is the way of the "unfit." Those directed to the right were going to be sent to hard labor, and the others—well, you just aren't sure, but it isn't long before you find out.

First, the SS soldiers rip the small suitcase from your arms— the one containing your infant—and toss it on a heap of other belongings. You scream and fight. You tell them to have mercy and shout through your panic, "My baby is in that suitcase!" A soldier looks at you with some sort of mocking compassion, unholsters his revolver, and unflinchingly shoots three bullets into the suitcase.

Someone nearby grabs you and supports you as you move forward in that massive line, downward, into what now appears to be a tunnel. There is wailing and sobbing, but there is no compassion. The SS soldiers are there to keep the line moving. One of them says, "What's all the fuss? You are simply going to take showers." That seems to quiet the crowd. The closer you get to the showers, the more the screams turn to silence—deadly silence. These are showers from which you will never return.

THE ATROCITIES

This is a typical Holocaust story; it is not overblown or dramatized for effect. It is what six million European Jews experienced, to a greater or lesser extent. It is unimaginable—history's worst genocide. Human beings were systematically and efficiently rounded up and methodically killed in death camps. There were heroes—far too few of them—who would hide Jews or help them to escape, thus putting their own lives on the line.

There were those who survived, who lived every day of their lives in terror of being found or caught; these people still have nightmares of the atrocities committed against their loved ones and the rapes and beatings they had to endure. One wonders if survival was the easiest way out. They are the witnesses, some still alive today, to tell the horrific stories of this shameful time in human history.

These atrocities too were prophesied almost 2,000 years earlier. As we see the gruesome pictures of bodies lying in a heap, the following scripture comes to mind:

"Your carcasses shall be food for all the birds of the air and the beasts of the earth, and no one shall frighten them away" (Deuteronomy 28:26).

It was the times that allowed such a horrendous undertaking. It was 1925 when Hitler published *Mein Kampf,* which was the propaganda used to incite hatred for the Jews in the thirties. Even conservative Roman Catholic and Protestant American clergy were heard railing against the Jews on the radio. There was a quota system imposed at many universities for the enrollment of Jews.

In 1933, Hitler came to power, and within two years, the Jews were no longer considered citizens. There were laws passed forcing Jews out of schools and jobs. In 1938, Jews were ordered to wear a yellow Star of David to identify them. The following year, the most hideous of all persecutions began—the Holocaust. It was 1945 before the Allied forces took over the death camps, but many Jews were still eliminated, especially in Poland in 1946.

The horror that plagued God's chosen people across the face of the earth for almost two millennia cannot be exaggerated or forgotten. The scattering and the persecution of the Jews were certainly predicted, but never did it ever give God any pleasure. They were His people and the "...apple of His eye" (Zechariah 2:8). The persecution was to make the Jews see what they had given up and drive them back to Israel.

THE INGATHERING

Chapter 36 of Ezekiel talks about the Lord "dispersing" the Jews. Verse 19 reads: "So I scattered them among the nations..." and verse 24 reads: "For I will take you from among the nations, gather you out of all countries, and bring you into your own land."

The Jews were exiled for nearly 2,000 years. This has been one of the most accurate, world-changing events of the last century. The impossible was brought into existence. All of those Bible scholars who worried about the Israel question were at once vindicated. Can you imagine living prior to 1948 and trying to make sense of the previous prophecy? Anyone reading this would probably have never believed it.

Against all odds, the nation of Israel was formed on May 14, 1948. To this day, Jews from other nations have been coming home, just as God promised. The gathering of the scattered people of Israel began when Israel became a nation. In 1947, the UN voted to partition Palestine into two separate states—one Jewish and one Arab.

There were the prophecies about the return, or the ingathering, of the Jews to their homeland, too. " ...I will gather you from the peoples, assemble you from the countries where you have been scattered, and I will give you the land of Israel" (Ezekiel 11:17).

The ingathering of the Jews has been an ongoing event since World War II. People were airlifted from all over Europe, North America, South America, Africa, and India.

The Bible says one pure language, Hebrew, must be spoken by the Jews (Zephaniah 3:9). Before 1948, this was a dead language. It's now spoken throughout Israel. Of course, the nation of Israel had to be reconstituted and Jerusalem brought under Jewish control, and this, too, has happened—no small feat.

The Ethiopian Jews must be returned to Israel (Zephaniah 3:10–11). There were a number of airlifts of Ethiopian Jews to Israel, carried out by the U.S. and Israel. Between 1977 and 1990; 15,000 were relocated in several airlift operations known as Operations Moses, Joshua, and Solomon.

There has to be an exodus of Russian Jews to the reborn Israeli state (Jeremiah 23:7–8). This took place in the seventies and eighties and continues today.

THE AGE WE LIVE IN

There were not many people living in the mid-twentieth century who believed that the Berlin Wall and the Iron Curtain would come tumbling down. Who could have foretold that terrorists from the Arab world would threaten our lives and disrupt world peace?

We are told about Ishmael through his father, Abraham, often referred to as the father of the Arab peoples. "He shall be a wild man; His hand shall be against every man, and every man's hand against him. And he shall dwell in the presence of his brethren" (Genesis 16:12). In the commentary of the previous scripture, it says, "Nothing can be more descriptive of the wandering lawless, freebooting life of the Arabs than this. From the beginning to the present they have kept their independence."

Who could have seen that Iraq, where the garden of Eden is thought to have been, could be a catalyst for World War III? How could the possibility of implanting computer chips into a human seem like anything but science fiction?

We somehow need to get out from under our personal complacency and realize that there is a grander scheme to this old world. This plan was set into motion thousands of years ago, and it will come to fruition regardless of our own petty ideas and ideals and regardless of what all men together should try to manipulate. This time on Earth can only end in one direction, and that is the way written down so long ago. How do we know? There is plenty to prove that which was once thought to be impossible prophecy has been fulfilled, and there is more to come. We need to learn how to read the signs of the times. There is no question that we are living our tomorrows—our future is now!

The prophetic scripture found in 2 Timothy is an accurate description of the age in which we live: "For men will be lovers of themselves, lovers of money, boasters, proud, blasphemers, disobedient to parents, unthankful, unholy" (2 Timothy 3:2).

"ME FIRST" GENERATION

Though the case may be made for other times in the past when these things have occurred, it was nowhere near as universal then as it is now. We Americans are living in the "me first" generation; there are few parameters and fewer morals. This is a worldwide catastrophe that has left many older people scratching their heads in bewilderment. There is such a contrast to other generations about what is socially and culturally acceptable.

We can accurately calculate our priorities and interests by simply observing how self-centeredness and arrogance rule this era. The absolute truth of God is being replaced with New Age beliefs and values that are most disconcerting. New Age centers around relativism and is almost universal in its scope. It embraces nearly every form of the occult and Eastern philosophies. It encourages self-centeredness couched in pleasant phrases like "self awareness." It is ultimately what almost everyone wants to hear—that we humans can and should be searching for only one thing, and that is the god within each of us.

Therefore, God has become an outcast, and those of us who love Him are disenfranchised. People, for the most part, are best described in the following passage of scripture concerning these end times.

> But know this, that in the last days perilous times will come:… unloving, unforgiving, slanderers, without self-control, brutal, despisers of good, traitors, headstrong, haughty, lovers of pleasures rather than lovers of God, having a form of godliness, but denying its power. And from such people turn away!
>
> 2 Timothy 3:1–5

This prophecy is being fulfilled every day. Wanting it all and wanting it yesterday have produced a generation where both parents work outside the home. That, in turn, has had a deleterious effect on the spoiled children who receive objects in place of love, time, and guidance. Guilt-ridden parents provide the latest toys for their children almost before they ask for them. Meanwhile, those children, while growing up, are ungrateful and disobedient, as the above passage reads. When fully grown, they become greedy and "lovers of pleasure more than lovers of God." The priorities have shifted, almost unknowingly, away from Christian living and toward instant self-gratification.

The fact is, however, that God has not changed, nor has the Bible. No matter how hard we try to blot out that line between right and wrong or good and evil, it still exists. No matter how hard we try to discredit the validity of the Bible, we cannot.

SIGNS OF THE TIMES

There has always been a lot of interest in the end times among the general public, but since this field has been at times dominated by deluded or—to be kind—overanxious folks, it's difficult to get a fair hearing. There are some Christians who have a strong interest in end-times prophecy because they enjoy the challenge of the Biblical symbolism, but these people are few in number. Most tend to back away from those sections in the Bible, especially in days gone by, when there was little to relate to in their particular era.

As a result, the history of end-times literature is littered with misinformation about what the Bible actually says on this topic. This leaves the field wide open for anyone who has some type of perceived insight. Thus, we have a host of failed attempts to describe or forecast what the last days on Earth may actually look like and when they might occur.

This is nothing new. For example, a farmer named William Miller convinced thousands of otherwise normal Americans that the world would come to an end between March 21, 1843, and March 21, 1844. As Miller traveled around the country delivering his message, many came to listen and jeer. At last count, he had about fifty thousand true believers and probably a million who were seriously interested. However, almost all were disappointed when the date came and went and nothing happened. He then moved the date to April 18, and when that passed Miller wrote, "I confess my error, and acknowledge my disappointment; yet I still believe that the day of the Lord is near, even at the door" (Bliss 1853, 256).

A small group led by James White came to the conclusion that Miller was right after all but had the wrong place. There was a big "purge" in heaven, and that was what Miller had mistakenly thought was the end of the world on Earth. This led to the establishment of the Seventh-Day Adventist Church as we know it today. Miller died a disappointed man, but his beliefs found a permanent home.

JESUS SPEAKS

In His Olivet discourse, below, Jesus responds to questions from His disciples concerning His second coming. There are seven major prophecies that need to be fulfilled before the tribulation and return of Christ in this passage of scripture.

Now as He sat on the Mount of Olives, the disciples came to Him privately, saying, "Tell us, when will these things be? And what will be the sign of Your coming, and of the end of the age?"

And Jesus answered and said to them, "Take heed that no one deceives you. For many will come in My name, saying, I am the Christ; and will deceive many. And you will hear of wars and rumors of wars. See that you are not troubled; for all these things must come to pass, but the end is not yet.

For nation will rise against nation, and kingdom against kingdom: and there will be famines, pestilences, and earthquakes, in various places. All these are the beginning of sorrows. Then they will deliver you up to tribulation, and kill you, and you will be hated by all nations for My name's sake. And then will many be offended, will betray one another, and will hate one another.

Then many false prophets will rise up and deceive many. And because lawlessness will abound, the love of many will grow cold. But he who endures to the end, shall be saved. And this gospel of the kingdom will be preached in all the world as a witness to all nations, and then the end will come."

Matthew 24:3–14

SEVEN FULFILLED PROPHECIES

FALSE "CHRISTS"

"Take heed that no one deceives you. For many will come in my name, saying, 'I am the Christ,' and will deceive many" (verses 4–5). His second coming will be characterized by an increasing number of these persons, who would have us believe a gospel other than that of the Bible. False teachers are often Christian cultists, those who twist the meaning of the Bible or perhaps even follow their own version written by a man. The apostles John and Paul also warned against these people. While things will get worse, the wheels have been set in motion, and we can count this prophecy fulfilled. Waco and Jonestown are just two examples.

WARS

"And you will hear of wars and rumors of wars. See that you are not troubled; for all these things must come to pass, but the end is not yet. For nation will rise against nation, and kingdom against kingdom" (verses 6–7a).

Wars are certainly nothing new; we have had them throughout recorded history. However, the number of wars seems to be on the increase in the first decade of the twenty-first century. Numbers vary depending on the definition of war and the source of the information. The UN defines a major war as a military conflict inflicting over one thousand battlefield deaths per year. In 2010 Global Security identified thirty-eight ongoing major and minor military conflicts worldwide. It's not so much the number of wars, but their characteristics that have changed. In World War I, civilian deaths amounted to about five percent of the total. Now, civilian deaths often outnumber military causalities.

Since the early nineties, the United States has been engaged in various conflicts in the Middle East. In 2010 we were engaged in major wars both in Iraq and Afghanistan. This generation has unprecedented threats of terrorism and nuclear war. Certainly, the world had never experienced anything like the loss of life in the first two world wars. These wars, fought primarily to decide who was going to rule a united Europe, were far greater in scope than any in the past. Estimates of those killed in World War I amount to about thirteen million, while World War II's deaths are estimated to be about fifty million. The next large war will involve weapons of mass destruction, and we can expect a much greater death toll—the final war, culminating in Armageddon.

FAMINES

"…And there will be famines…" (verse 7).

Even though food is plentiful, there are those who are still dying from starvation. Famine is widespread across Africa. As Christian farmers were pushed out of Africa, they were replaced by those who took out important food crops and planted poppies—the source of illegal drugs such as heroin. While many are starving to death, these unscrupulous people supply twenty-five percent of the world's illegal drugs. India and many of its neighbors have also had food shortages for many years.

The latest UN statistics on agriculture and global warming indicate that roughly one-fifth of the earth's population goes hungry every day. Food aid workers are attacked by armed soldiers in areas such as Darfur, in Africa. Global warming, plus poor land usage and residential development, have reduced the amount of farmland worldwide, and the population of the world continues to increase, especially in those areas where the growth in agriculture has declined.

Basic, good farming practices, such as holding land fallow for a season and crop rotation, are hard to follow if you don't know about them or you are constantly hungry.

In 2008, many of the poorer areas of Africa, Asia, and Latin America experienced famine. Part of this resulted from the rapid and unexpected growth in grain commodity prices. Global Research reported in April 2008 that the most popular grade of Thailand's rice sold for $198 a ton in 2003. It was $323 a ton in 2007, and it was about $1,000 in March 2008. As a result, food riots have taken place in Haiti, Egypt, the Ivory Coast, Bolivia, Mexico, Peru, Indonesia, the Philippines, Pakistan, Uzbekistan, Thailand, Yemen, Ethiopia, and in many other sub-Saharan African nations.

In June 2009 the United Nations announced that world hunger "hit one billion." The number increased by one hundred million over the year before. There were fifty famines in the world in the years 2001–2009 (Mapreport.com 2010, 1).

PESTILENCE

" ...Pestilences ... " (verse 7)

We have new plagues that have never been known before. In our society of global travel, we have never had a widespread, high death toll resulting from a disease outbreak, but the Center for Disease Control thinks such a pandemic is possible, if not likely.

Part of the problem today is that diseases of the past, previously thought to be under control, are now on the upsurge. These include malaria, tuberculosis, and polio. Despite many breakthroughs, AIDS is still ravaging the human body and continues to spread, especially in Africa, where it has assumed epidemic proportions in some areas. There was the bird flu, which claimed the lives of fifty percent of its victims over the age of sixty-five. Then SARS, a deadly respiratory disease, seemingly exploded out of China and reached epidemic status in 2003.

H1N1 swine flu was predicted to reach epidemic proportions in 2009; it infected mostly children and pregnant women and fortunately was better contained than first anticipated. There are even horrible flesh-eating diseases like Ebola with various outbreaks in Africa and fatality rates as high as 53 percent in the Sudan in 2002. What mutates tomorrow may just make this writing obsolete. Our technology cannot seem to stay ahead of pestilence.

MRSA—methicillin-resistant *Staphylococcus aureus*—is a superbug that started to spread in institutional environments in 2007 and 2008. This infection is most commonly found in jails and hospitals, but it has now spread to schools. When treated immediately, this infection can be cured, but once it enters the body and becomes systemic, it cannot be treated with antibiotics; it is immune to them.

In addition, other forms of drug-resistant bacteria, like staph infections, are found in greater concentrations in hospitals than in the past. Some forms of these drug-resistant infections are even immune to the caustic cleaners that are commonly used in institutional settings.

EARTHQUAKES AND TRIBULATION

"...and earthquakes in various places..." (verse 7).

The number of earthquakes occurring has increased, and even with all of our technology, thousands of people are dying. In 2003, *CNN Headline News* suddenly announced that over 2,200 people died in an earthquake in Algeria and that another 10,000 were injured. An underwater earthquake near Indonesia created tsunami waves that were reported to have killed 220,000 persons in Asia and Africa in 2004.

Volcanologists and our news media report that the incidence of earthquakes has increased in recent years. Up until the 1950s, killer quakes "averaged two to four a decade" (Lindsay 1997, 296). Today, there are so many that they count the number of world-wide earthquakes in terms of days or weeks.

In contrast, between the years 1890 and 1900, there was only one major earthquake recorded in the entire world. Experts in biblical prophecy state that there is no doubt that the increasing incidence of earthquakes at such an alarming pace is one of the signs of the end times—that period marked by the final days of the church age and the ushering in of the seven-year tribulation.

For example, for the seven days ending November 20, 2008, there were a total of 263 earthquakes worldwide that measured at least 2.5 on the Richter scale. Many of these were above the 4.0 mark, where major damage is likely to occur. In the first few months of 2010 there were ten major earthquakes. In January, after being hit by a 7.0 magnitude quake, over one hundred thousand people were killed and over one million were left homeless in Haiti. In February Chile was hit with an 8.8

magnitude quake, one of the strongest ever recorded. In April a major earthquake hit Tibet.

In the past, we thought we knew where earthquakes were likely to strike, and we could take proper precautions like strict building codes. Now the scientific community has discovered that inter-plate earthquakes are also possible. Not only do we not know where these are unless they have occurred in the past, but they are much more dangerous.

Those earthquakes on the plate edges have some of their energy absorbed in the fractured rock from previous quakes. Thus, an earthquake in a mid-plate location (for example, New York City) would find a relatively small reading on the Richter scale to be a major disaster. While infrequent, these mid-plate quakes do occur, and since there is a general increase in all earthquakes, it can be assumed there will be more of these, as Jesus said, "in various places."

PERSECUTION

"All these are the beginning of sorrows. Then shall they deliver you up to tribulation and kill you, and you be will be hated by all nations for my name's sake" (verse 8,9).

Throughout the world, Christians are under attack. In Russia, China, North Korea, Africa, and most of the Muslim countries, Christians are imprisoned and even killed daily, though we hear little of it here.

On October 26, 2008, the Pope called for an end to the killing of Christians in India and Iraq. In India, anti-Christian riots by Hindu extremists had claimed thirty-eight lives since August

2008 and destroyed dozens of churches, leaving as many as thirty thousand homeless. According to the UN, Sunni extremists chased some thirteen thousand Christians out of their homes in northern Iraq in 2008. The Pope asked national authorities to put a stop to both of these situations.

The United States has had its share of persecution of Christians as well. While many still go to church on Sunday, it is more out of tradition than faith. Christianity is vilified in our media and often by the actions of those who are the stars of our society. Finally, there's the hidden agenda of the New Age Movement, which eventually calls for the elimination of Christians and Jews alike.

SO CLOSE

"And this gospel of the kingdom will be preached in all the world as a witness to all the nations, and then shall the end come" (verse 14).

It wasn't long ago, even with all of our expertise, that we still had a portion of the earth that we could not reach via TV, radio, or missionaries. It was called the 10/40 window because it referred to those regions of the eastern hemisphere located between 10 and 40 degrees north of the equator.

The term was coined by a Christian missionary in 1990 to delineate those areas in the Saharan and Northern Africa, as well as almost all of Asia. These regions were characterized by poverty, lack of access to Christian resources, and government opposition due to the predominance of other religions. With the advent of computers, the Internet, and satellite TV, people all over the world can now hear the message of the gospel.

Those countries that do not allow Christian evangelists within their borders can now be reached from the outside by modern technology. Today, the Bible is readily translated into even the most obscure dialects with relative ease. The wireless revolution gives evangelists one more tool.

Afghanistan and Iraq are two recent areas formerly difficult to reach that are now more accessible to Christian outreach. Hopefully, more will follow, as much of the Arab world is dragged, kicking and screaming, from the the seventh century AD—Mohammed's death—into the twenty-first century. Unfortunately, the Bible and the cross are banned in such a society, as are all non-Islamic books and icons.

One remaining missionary issue is that literacy is a major problem in areas where the Bible is still not widely available. Modern missionaries are finding it is necessary to not only translate the Bible into local dialects but to teach many how to read it. Thus, we can see that while the fulfillment of this prophecy is at hand, it has not yet completely happened. There are also areas of the undeveloped world where small villages have no electricity. However, you can see we are very close to the end. People have been looking to prophecy through the ages for Christ's return, but it is those of us who are living now on a countdown to eternity. That is exciting news.

MORE PROPHECY

There is more to prophecy than the seven listed above. Much has happened or is in the process of coming into being. From our (Christian) vantage point, we can look at additional prophecies and draw some conclusions about where this world of ours is headed. This all does not have to be taken on faith. You will walk through it on many levels: spiritually, practically, historically, logically, and scientifically.

Don't forget the Olivet events are like birth pangs—as they occur, we can expect them to get worse and faster until the crescendo is reached: the rapture and the tribulation. Scripture does not tell us exactly how long the birth pangs will take, but there may be other clues that will help us there.

Revelation 9:14–16 tells us there will be an army of 200 million men in the east. No nation in history had ever had an army of this size, but since the sixties, China has had one, according to Chairman Mao (Lindsay 1970). Since no country would use all of its troops in a foreign operation, a possible Muslim coalition of forces would more than make up the difference.

In addition, Russia must be a strong nation for certain end-times scenarios. Russia's conversion to a capitalistic economic system will strengthen what is already a powerful military state. As an oil-exporting nation, Russia has benefitted from the dramatic rise in crude oil prices. The long-term economic picture favors all oil-exporting nations, and even at lower prices, oil is not only money—it is power.

MAKING IT HAPPEN

In the past, the problem with many end-times prophecies was that something was read into scripture that just wasn't there. Forcing a fulfilled tag on prophecy was done by well-meaning folks who were a little overanxious. Many people tended to ascribe symbolic meaning to something that should be read for its clear, common-sense meaning. There are places where the wording is symbolic, but that is not the norm.

The reason for this problem was that the requirements for the end times just didn't seem to make sense to past generations. Things needed to happen over the course of time. Inventions needed to be invented, and technology needed to advance. People didn't always get it, and when things didn't seem to point in the right direction, they felt they had to help things along by imposing their own interpretation, since the stated prophecies seemed impossible.

For example, if you lived one hundred years ago, would you be ready to accept the idea of a 200 million-man army? Even stranger, would you believe that the nation of Israel, dead for about 1,800 years, would be reborn? How about worldwide communication and television or computer chips that would facilitate the implanting of the mark of the beast? As these prophecies and others seemed unlikely, it was reasonable to assume that all prophecies should be read as symbolic when they were usually meant to be clear statements of unfulfilled fact.

There are also many other areas of fulfilled prophecy in the Bible that have nothing to do with end times or with the second coming of Christ. The Dead Sea Scrolls took away any doubt about when these prophecies were written. They fix the Old Testament prophecies at a time of about 100 BC; there is no significant disagreement about this date. All of the prophecies about the birth, life, and death of Jesus Christ took place well before his birth.

THE STAGE IS SET

It is exciting to live at a time when all things seem to be coming together and prophecy makes sense—when everything is in place to make that which has been foretold come true. There are no more inventions that must be invented, no more wars that must be fought, and no more cryptic messages to which we don't relate. Everything is ready; the stage is set for a military and administrative genius such as Napoleon. At its height, the Napoleonic Empire included all of western and central Europe, excepting Portugal, Great Britain, and Sweden. Austria and Prussia were allied with him by treaty.

Bismarck united Germany in the nineteenth century and forged treaties with other powerful countries in Europe like Austria, Italy, and Russia. His dream of a united Europe under the control of Germany led, at least in part, to World War I.

Of course, over the centuries, many military leaders tried to conquer Europe from the outside. These attacks, including the Muslim invasions, all failed. It is interesting to note that, with the exception of Napoleon, all the internal efforts listed were those of Germanic leaders. The loss of World War I temporarily ended the idea of a Germanic-speaking, united Europe until a new leader burst onto the scene—Adolf Hitler.

From the fall of the Roman Empire to the formation of the European Union, the dream of many was to reunite Europe. This was attempted by force and by political union. A few made significant progress for a time, but in the end, their work was in vain. Unfortunately, this dream caused tremendous loss of life over the centuries—an especially ironic lesson in that the dream was only finally achieved by peaceful, political—not military—means. The apt description of the Roman Empire (and therefore Europe) by Daniel is a combination of iron and clay, substances that do not mix well.

With history as their incentive and prophecy at the helm, the affairs of men began to fit into the plans of God—prophecies that just decades ago seemed impossible. However, most Christians are oblivious to what's going on spiritually. We sit in pews every Sunday and leave any knowledge behind when we exit as though it isn't real or pertinent. We do surmise that the arrogance and self-centeredness discussed in 2 Timothy plays a role in these last days, but Christians fail to recognize it in our own society. If we were really in touch with God and His plan, we would be much more able to perceive the future.

THE SPIRIT REALM

Christians, like everyone else, have a lot to learn or at least understand, when it comes to the supernatural. First, you should know that Satan exists, and he knows the Bible quite well. In fact, he often seduces man by twisting the Bible just slightly, but in such a way as to draw a conclusion that he would like us to reach and one with which we are comfortable. In his audacity, he even tried to tempt Jesus with his corruption of the Word (Matthew 4:1–11).

Satan realizes his time is limited and that his best plan is to place one of his own in charge of the most powerful economic unit on Earth—the European Union, or the reborn Roman Empire (Daniel 9:26). Then, his plan will be exactly as laid out in the Bible. The antichrist, or the head of the European Union, taken over by Satan himself with the support of the false prophet, will bring the whole world under his sway.

Satan is an imitator, not a creator, and thus we will see many areas where he has copied things that God has done. You can see Satan, the antichrist, and the false prophet become a reproduction of the Trinity. There is a plot in place, and it will move forward. With the aid of history, scripture, and logic, a time line will be set.

There will be many uniting forces to bring Satan's plan to fruition. They will all come together to present a seamless world with a masterful leader. Everything will fit under the same umbrella: governments, politics, economics, philosophies, and religions. The religion of the end times will be all-inclusive and very flexible. It will embrace the masses, and it will appear to be the answer the world has been searching for. It will be backed by very important people and organizations, and its focus will seemingly be on love and world peace.

CHAPTER TWO:

THE NEW AGE IS UPON US

A RELIGION, A MOVEMENT,
A POLITICAL STAND—

THE NEW AGE IS OLD AGE
WHOSE TIME IS AT HAND.

This chapter is not about the innocent, amusing diversion your mind might conger up when you hear the term New Age. This is a philosophy as well as a religion. It is conveniently couched in strange terminology and Christian sounding words and phrases.

Historians think of Helena Blavatsky, born in the Russian Empire in 1831 and died in London in 1891, as the modern founder of the New Age religion. She combined oriental "wisdom" (or philosophies) with the occult and was a founder of the Theosophical Society. She was most controversial and important with her New Age ideologies. She was a prolific writer and some of her books are referred to as "The Collected Works" by her followers. Blavatsky called "the God of Abraham, Isaac, and Jacob a spiteful and revengeful deity" (Blavatsky 1888, 439).

There are two very basic questions that must be answered to have any grasp of this complicated philosophy: What makes New Age religion a religion, and who is their god? Religion has become a very generic term in today's society. Loosely stated, religion is a set of beliefs and doctrines with a purpose, having devout followers. As far as the god of the New Age well, he is really just an energy force that is everywhere and nowhere and in everything and in every non-thing. This godhood includes people—with or without bodies—animals, objects, planets, stars, and unseen energies, as well as nirvana or the great void—where "all is absorbed in the spirit of the most Powerful, and individual consciousness and activity cease" (Blatvatsky 1866, 196).

This "religion" traces its roots back to the second-century Gnostics. Since they believed they had special knowledge about God, they purposely confused outsiders by spouting nonsense.

Articles or books by Creme, Bailey, Muller, and other proponents of the New Age, couch their true philosophy in so much gobbledygook that little is to be learned. Robert Muller, the Under-Secretary General of the United Nations, wrote, "Global education must prepare our children for a planetary age" (Muller 1982, 8). This will lay the groundwork for a One-World Government and a One-World Religion. The ultimate unification of the world's religions is the goal of the New Age. "The new religion will manifest, for instance, through organizations like masonry. In Freemasonry is embedded the core or the secret heart of the occult mysteries, wrapped up in number, metaphor, and symbol" (Crème 1980, 87).

THEIR "GODS"

The Hierarchy of spiritual entities of this movement is huge, complex, and difficult to unscramble. Here, only two spiritual entities of New Age will be described. You will immediately recognize the clever twists on Christianity. The first is the god who represents the Hierarchy to man, and his name is Maitreya the Christ. For you who may not know, the term "Christ" is not a name, but more of a title meaning "The Anointed One." At important times in history, Maitreya chose Hermes, Zoroaster, Orpheus, and Jesus as his vehicles.

The next god is the top dog. His name is Lucifer, which means "light bearer." Lucifer, of course, is the name of Satan before the fall. In the beginning, he lived in heaven and was *the* angel among angels. The New Agers call him "the anointed cherub who was in the garden of Eden." We know that in the garden of Eden, he was Satan—not Lucifer—and he manifested himself as a serpent.

Because of the stigma attached to his name, Lucifer allows men to call him Krishna, Buddha, or Christ/Messiah. New Agers say that this being is symbolized by these names and others in many cultures, which neatly ties Eastern philosophies to Satan. The ultimate goal of the New Age plan is "planetary initiation," over which Lucifer rules. He is also in charge of human evolution. Planetary initiation is what many describe as the New World Order or simply "The Plan," the day when all this falls into place.

Before you dismiss this remember that one of the major things New Agers are counting on is that we do not take them seriously. The New Age is most influential in our society today. You will find it embedded deeply into our politics, economy, and our educational system.

"One of the biggest advantages we have as New Agers, we have concepts that are very acceptable to the general public. So we can change the names [and] open the door to millions" (Sutphen 1986, 14). If you think that's an exaggeration, read on and see just how successful they have been in reaching their goals.

WHO IS ALICE BAILEY?

Most American parents would be very surprised to know that their children are being taught New Age groupthink principles, as well as other New Age philosophies, in their public schools. It's not by chance, but rather by careful planning, meticulous timing, and supernatural intervention—and not by God.

A prolific writer on mysticism and the founder of an international esoteric movement, Alice Bailey was born in England. After a sheltered upbringing, she did evangelical work with the British Army, which took her to India. In 1907, she married Walter Evans, and they immigrated to America, where he became an Episcopalian minister. The marriage failed, and after the birth of three daughters, she obtained a divorce.

In America, she discovered the works of Madam Blavatsky and became active in the Theosophical Society. Blavatsky's *Secret Doctrine* of occult masters led her, in 1919, to the occult spirit Djual Khool. Bailey penned a series of books, which she claims the Tibetan, whose name she spelled "Djwhal Khul," dictated to her through an inner voice and which she wrote down word for word.

"The Tibetan has asked me to make clear that when he is speaking of the Christ he is referring to His official name as Head of the Hierarchy. The Christ works for all men irrespective of their faith; He does not belong to the Christian world anymore than the Buddhist the Mohammedan or any other faith. There is no need for any man to join the Christian Church in order to be affiliated with Christ" (Bailey 1957, 558).

In 1920, Alice married another Theosophist, Foster Bailey, and in 1923 they started the Arcane School to teach disciples how to further the Great Universal Plan under the guidance of the inner hierarchy of spiritual masters led by Christ. After her death, the school was carried on by her husband.

During her lifetime Alice Bailey studied Madam Blavatsky writings and went on to publish twenty-five of her own works in fifty languages for those interested in the New Age and the occult. Her work continued to influence the New Age movement as well as those who came after her such as Muller and Creme.

NEW AGE IN EDUCATION

Alice Bailey was a self-proclaimed occultist whose doctrine is already in schools internationally, including the U.S. She died in 1949, yet her books and teachings are still considered irreplaceable by those who follow the New Age movement. It is her writings that have been carefully integrated into our school system. Ms. Bailey's education outline centers around the goal of "the smooth functioning of the One Humanity." Her major doctrines include "groupthink", "values clarification," "behavior modification" and relativism—no absolutes. By the way, this is a slow, gradual process that best begins in infancy when little minds are so moldable. And as the child grows, so does the level of indoctrination.

When Bill Clinton was Governor of Arkansas, he instituted an optional summer school program for seventeen-year-olds with above-average IQs and potential. In "The Ominous Success of Re-Education" by Berit Kjos (October 5, 2009), he presents information concerning Governor Bill Clinton's "Governor's School" that lasted six weeks each summer. Here is a typical speaker comment, "Students do me a favor. Totally ignore your parents. Listen to them, then forget them." The aim of this speaker was to free students from "obsolete" family values. They were to become open-minded ready to accept heretofore unthinkable practices. Among others, they studied the gay lifestyle and the premise of there being no such thing as absolute truth.

The Clinton school was modeled after the North Carolina Governor's School. Luther Setzer is a self-proclaimed atheist who attended that North Carolina School in 1982. He was particularly outraged by some of the claims made about Eugenics. "While I remain an atheist, I can sympathize with religious folks who resent having their tax money spent to teach values contrary to their own" (Setzer 2010, 2).

NEW AGE THINKING

This program is a perfect template of the current NA thinking with regard to education. First, the students are to be isolated to the greatest extent possible from all authority figures, especially parents. They are then instructed to look for the god within themselves for ideas. These ideas, no matter how bizarre, can be presented to the class.

The class may decide which ones to embrace, and that will be an acceptable outcome. An appropriate outcome might be that there is no need for any of these college-bound students to go to college. Taken to a further extreme, the taking of lives of fellow students might also be an acceptable outcome. This program, initiated in 1979, is still in operation in Arkansas. Similar programs are found in other states such as Washington and Oregon, and even in some private schools.

If this reminds you of the book *1984*, by George Orwell, you are right on target. The disturbing thing is that while any reasonable person could see the error of groupthink in Orwell's book, it seems that the U.S. Department of Education and the UN cannot. Since the mid-nineties, the UN has distributed to its member nations their worldwide-recommended educational curriculum. For all practical purposes, this is largely taken from Alice Bailey's *Education for a New Age*, on the subject. The input of groupthink and rejection of authority are major components of the UN program.

OBE

Part of a resolution approved by the Southern Baptist Convention in June 1994 reads as follows: "Whereas, many parents are concerned that Outcome-Based Education de-emphasizes traditional academic instruction basic academic skills such as reading, writing, and arithmetic in favor of how students feel about things and promote multiculturalism, in 'politically correct' social values and New Age philosophies to the exclusion of traditional Judeo-Christian values. Therefore, Be it resolved, That we, the messengers to the Southern Baptist Convention...oppose educational reform experiments including those labeled 'Outcome-Based Education,' which risks the undermining of Judeo-Christian values, local control and traditional academic standards of excellence" (SBC.net 1994, 1).

Not only are children being exposed to New Age concepts under the broad title of Outcome-Based Education (OBE). These students are told not to relate any of this nonsense to their parents, and most do not. According to *Elementary School Guidance Counseling Journal* (April 1981) OBE has the following function: "To create 'cognitive dissonance' in children age 5 and up. They are then to withhold adult input to force reliance on an answer acceptable to the peer group. Its purpose is to remodel the entire political, economic and social structure (as well as individual) identity." As there is no traditional authority accepted in the New Age educational program that must be observed, children are instructed to find the god within themselves for answers. But more alarming than this is the fact that some students are actually taking classes that glorify death. That may well lead to the taking of lives—perhaps fellow students as well as their own. In case you think that this is an exaggeration, Columbine High School in Littleton, Colorado, had such a curriculum.

OBE offers classes on death, dying, and suicide. Tara Backer, a student at Columbine High School, was interviewed by Tom Jarrel for ABC 's 20/20 program in 1988. Tara said that the morbid focus on death at the school led to her and others attempting suicide. As part of the death program, students visited cemeteries and embalming labs. *Atlantic Monthly* confirmed this at Columbine and other schools in an investigative article done in 1988 (The 20/20 program aired September 21, 1990; The Atlantic Monthly 1988, 30).

BE AWARE, INFORMED, AND ALERT

The U.S. is more difficult to influence than many other nations, as we do not take well to new ideas that sound strange. In this case, our natural nativism stands us in good stead. However, the

U.S. Department of Education has managed to get "Goals 2000" and "No Child Left Behind" passed, courtesy of Presidents Clinton and G.W. Bush, respectively both of which embrace OBE principles. So today many of our public schools, promote New Age ideas and philosophies.

We should never forget that this altering of mind-sets is the same type of thinking that allowed SS Nazis to exterminate millions of Jews and others deemed to be inferior. Himmler, the man Hitler put in charge of the Final Solution, built a castle to his design to worship the gods of the New Age.

If you think that New Age is just a harmless thing that involves crystals and some Eastern practices such as reincarnation, you should immediately reexamine this opinion. New Age is presented to you courtesy of the group that brought you the Holocaust, and is believed to be the religion of the coming antichrist.

The New Age message and intent is not as innocuous as it appears on the surface. Rather, it is a surreptitious indoctrination that undermines all Christian values and morals and puts a great divide between generations.

A MIX AND MATCH RELIGION

This religion is so eclectic that there is something for everybody. Energy, forces, karma, and mantra are shamelessly taken from other religions and are buzzwords for New Agers. As confusing as this whole plot gets, it provides the desired results, and that is that parents get tired of trying to wade through this non-language, so they give up. This allows these people to have their own way; it accomplishes exactly what it set out to do. It remains an enigma to most, but to those who are plotting to change our destinies by first changing our schools, it all makes perfect sense: start with the youth and be patient.

People are in place already, as many New Age philosophies and concepts are already in our school systems. These are the same people who put values clarification, behavior modification, situational ethics, and no right or wrong—relativism—in our schools. This plan, in case you didn't get it, is how Ms. Bailey saw global education; remember that hers is still the goal today for New Agers. She expressed her ideal as being reached through bridge building. The goal hasn't changed over the years; it teaches youngsters how to meld into one humanity.

If you do an Internet search for "New Age" and do not understand much on the sites, you are in good company, but it cannot be stressed enough that this is intentional on the part of New Agers. They purposely say things in riddles or codes. They take many of their names and titles from ancient pagan gods, and they throw in some good-sounding Christian buzzwords.

New Agers add Eastern religions and philosophies and occult movements and blend it all together. Most terms that would be unfamiliar take on a dark and powerful meaning when used by those in leadership. There are many in their own movement who cannot know certain truths, so this deliberate double-talk takes care of that problem.

A SUBTLE INDOCTRINATION

It's interesting to note that it is often the intellectual elite who fall hardest for anything that spells change. This is certainly the case in education. Part of it stems from the great pride they take in the myriads of diplomas hanging from their walls. There's just no way to admit that they don't understand something, and it seems like nothing can be too extreme or liberal. Isn't this the same breed of people who, for decades, has been banning God and prayer in schools? Aren't they the ones whose bright idea it was to pass out condoms to seventh and eighth graders? Aren't they the same people who fought for abortions for teens without parental knowledge or consent?

People in this country really get up in arms when they have their sovereignty threatened, their right to bear arms, or their freedom of speech—which they should—yet they turn over their children for daily indoctrination into New Age philosophies. When all is said and done, we're all getting hurt and duped by these doctrines. Parents and children suddenly have very different values. Desensitizing young people to morals and individual thinking is creating a new generation of impersonal humans, and that, too, is by design.

Why has this implantation into our education system been so smooth and easy? Deception is just that—subtle and usually undetectable. We are all prideful enough to believe we will know deceit when it enters our lives. Besides which, we all tend to trust the "experts," which can be a mistake. Often, the teachers are as poorly informed as we are as to the true agenda and are just following orders.

There is much in Ms. Bailey's writings and plans that stresses good over evil and even love, so with a cursory glance, everything seems right, and unfortunately that's all most of us do; that's all most parents have the time to do. For the more diligent parents, when they have their turn to speak out, they are deemed as overreacting, so they pull their kids out and put them into private schools. You should know that Alice Bailey's definition of love is "a group relationship, in order that knowledge should be subordinated to the group need and interest."

There are those who are fighting Outcome-Based Education both here and in Europe, citing illiteracy and other shortcomings. This is good, but are these people aware of the New Age connection and exactly what that means? It is bad enough having a system in place that is not effective, but it is far worse to trace back its roots to some bizarre channeler whose main purpose is to create little robots of our children who cannot think for themselves.

THE PLAN

Education is only a part of the plan—a socio-economic, political, education plan—of the New Age, which has been in the offing for some time now. It was carefully put together to be seamlessly placed into the world. All preparations have been made. New Agers must submit to the plan or be left out of the New World Order. They believe that this plan, written by Alice Bailey, was dictated to her by a supernatural entity—the Tibetan master Djwhal Khul. The purpose of the plan is to get mankind to their "next evolutionary level" in order to be able to begin the new "Root Race." However, it appears that the plan is far simpler than that; it is to get the world ready for One-World Government, which will raise the curtain on the antichrist.

One of the foremost tenets of this plan is to institute a new world religion, getting rid of organized religion as we now know it—especially Judaism, and eventually Christianity. The Hierarchy will make an appearance on Earth to reveal this new, universal religion, which of course will be the New Age religion. It may have a different name; it may even sound like the answer to world peace. This is the NA scenario relating to the end times as depicted in the Bible.

It must be understood that any quote taken from the founders of this movement, either Alice Bailey or H.P. Blavatsky, which refer to "Christ" is by their own admission any of many entities including Satan or Lucifer. "Satan is the god of our planet, and the only god" (Blavatsky 1884, 234).

Alice Bailey writes, "Prepare men for the reappearance of the Christ. This is your first and greatest duty" (Bailey 1957, 641). Also, "Forgetting the things that lie behind, I will strive towards my higher spiritual possibilities. I dedicate myself anew to the service of the Coming One (antichrist/Lucifer) and will do all I can to prepare men's minds and hearts for that event..." (Bailey 1955, 641).

AN ANSWER FOR EVERYTHING

When master manipulators twist words, telling people what they want to hear, the masses believe them. While Judaism remains a target, as in Nazi Germany, Christianity, it seems, will be used in a very subtle distortion to the Bible. As you know, in the last days there will be a rapture of the church. Most Christians believe that this will allow the antichrist his time on Earth.

Well, New Agers have cleverly twisted the meaning of these scripture passages. As part of their plan, those who do not believe in New Age will be ousted from the earth by their evil Shamballa force. According to them, the church is not taken out of the earth leading to the second coming of Christ; instead, the nonbelievers will have been ejected from the planet so that the New World Order can finally become a total unified reality.

Of course, the truth is that their leader, the Son of Perdition, cannot come to power as long as the church is on this planet. However, with the saints and the Holy Spirit no longer on Earth, evil will be allowed to proliferate. The explanation of the New Agers is really quite brilliant.

It neatly puts to rest any loose ends left dangling from the disappearance of millions of people. At the same time, it shines the spotlight on the New Age and their fulfilled prophecy of the nonbelievers being ejected from the planet. It also strengthens their position considerably. It injects a fear factor, which says to those left, "If you don't line up with our doctrine, we have the power to eject you from the earth." That's quite an incentive to join the new faith and toe the line. Clever—diabolically clever!

Meanwhile, "The Hierarchy waits. The Christ (antichrist/Lucifer) stands in patient silence, attentive to the effort that will make His work materialize on Earth…The Buddha hovers over the planet, ready to play His part if mankind offers the opportunity to Him" (Bailey 1948, 38).

However, there is what's real and powerful, like God Almighty, and then there is a copy. The copy can do no more than pretend and present scenarios based on those pretensions. Satan is and always was the master copier. He can act like God and perhaps even look like God, but he will always be a loser. For those of you who have not read the Bible, turn to the end—we win! Christians leaving this planet will not be ejected, but instead, there will be a "catching up" into heaven.

"Then we who are alive and remain shall be caught up together with them in the clouds to meet the Lord in the air" (1 Thessalonians 4:17).

EVER-EVOLVING

The purpose of the New Age, it seems, is for humans to evolve spiritually until we rediscover the god in each of us. They believe in reincarnation and karma—concepts borrowed from Eastern religions. They also adhere to the practices of meditation and yoga. There is no central headquarters or even a central figure in this religion.

There is an invitation by Lucifer into the New Age. Then, the initiated must reach a point of illumination. Their goal is the conclusion that "all is one" must be reached. As far as the antichrist is concerned, New Agers say he is not a person, but rather a destructive energy force let loose to break down the old world order. It seems their New World Order will greatly resemble Hitler's Europe—if Hitler had won.

If you doubt their resolve or their large numbers, just log onto the Internet and type in the words "New Age." If you still think that they are not a force to be reckoned with, notice that they have infiltrated every segment of society, politics, and religion. There are New Age magazines and newspapers, books and stores. There are New Age gifts, art, and music. They have cleverly infused our language with terms that once may have been foreign or even offensive but are now quite comfortable. They have taken that one step further by the introduction of New Age practices into our everyday lives.

YOGA

There are areas of the New Age that we don't necessarily connect with that movement, which once again speaks to the
subtlety of it. For instance, while going through our local paper,
I came across a three-quarter page advertisement for nurses. In
order to encourage nurses to work in one particular hospital, they
were advertising the "Nursing Oasis." The copy read, in part, "It's a
peaceful environment of art, music, and tranquility, where nurses
can go before, during, and after work to relax and rejuvenate."

Sounds great! The very large picture that accompanied the
ad was of a very attractive woman—nurse?—in a black leotard,
sitting in the "lotus" position with her eyes closed. Does anyone
know what that's called? It's called yoga.

The dictionary defines yoga as "a mystic and ascetic Hindu
discipline by which one seeks to achieve liberation of the self
and union with the supreme spirit or universal soul through
intense concentration, deep meditation, and practices involving
prescribed postures, controlled breathing, etc." (Webster's New
World College Dictionary, 2009).

Actually, in the Hindu religion, there is no one supreme
being; they believe in millions of impersonal gods. The word
"yoga" comes from a term that means "to unite." The real purpose
of it is to bring yourself into union with the impersonal god—
the divine force, or, to put it another way, the true goal of yoga
is one of self-realization or enlightenment. Enlightenment is a
term Buddha used while searching for nirvana, or the god within
himself. That is exactly how New Agers see it—finding the god
within yourself. You can practice yoga all you want, but don't kid
yourself about what it means.

WESTERN YOGA-AN OXYMORON

According to recent polls, over sixteen million Americans practice yoga—an increase of over forty-three percent since 2002. Today, there are many forms of yoga. There is yoga for the expectant mother and for her newborn baby. There is yoga to deal with stress and sagging muscles. The greatest oxymoron of all is Christian yoga. Yoga is "medicine" for the body and mind, and most serious practitioners are looking for and finding a connection to themselves. The problem is that when all is said and done, this is an ancient Hindu philosophy that has become a serious part of the New Age Movement. Searching for an inner self, or enlightenment, is exactly what Buddhism and New Age have set as a goal. Looking for the best of you can eventually lead to perfection, or nirvana.

What is wrong with this? Well, we were created to not be self-centered and self-absorbed, but rather to be God-centered, and this practice clearly puts you in the center of your universe. This is a place reserved for God, and when we meditate, we should be meditating on God's Word and His will. Becoming all we are in Him should be the object for every Christian.

However, you will not find many who practice yoga who think it's any more than a breathing, exercise, or relaxation technique. People would laugh at you for suggesting that it might be connected to a religion, and even those who admit that perhaps it once was are adamant that there's no religion in it for them. Yoga is one of those wonderful, smorgasbord practices that has something for everyone and cleverly masquerades as a simple exercise regime.

FENG SHUI

If you're inclined to think that yoga is just one case of New Age-ism in our society, how about *feng shui?* Many believe it is simply the trendy method of placing furniture. If you're a little more knowledgeable, it is a way of achieving harmony between humans and their environment. Literally, the words translate from the Chinese to "wind-water," and in some circles it is known as the art of placement.

Actually, it is far more than furniture placement. It is a complicated philosophy that needs to be called to your attention by giving you a very broad definition. It is a metaphysical science and an ancient Chinese art that is about five thousand years old. It was absorbed into Buddhism and today is widely practiced by Westerners as part of the New Age Movement. Just how many are practicing these things while believing them to be non-religious? In other words, how many are totally unaware and ignorant of the true meanings of these seemingly benign practices? How many don't care?

Feng shui deals with *chi,* or life force. This is the energy that is the driving force behind the universe. In *feng shui,* one is contacting this *chi* to gain harmony in all endeavors, especially in manmade structures. The operative word here is "force"—that is the term used for New Age entities.

The two practices of yoga and *feng shui* were addressed several years ago by the Vatican; this shows how prevalent these practices are. The bottom line of the article is that it mentions yoga and *feng shui* as "occult, New Age practice(s) that emphasizes 'being in tune with nature or the cosmos'." Cardinal Paul Poupard, head of the Pontifical Council for culture, said, "I want to say simply that the New Age presents itself as a false utopia in answer to the profound thirst for happiness in the human heart" (BBC News, Tuesday February 4, 2003). In a typical, let's-not-offend-anyone way, the Vatican seemed to be saying, "Don't go near this stuff!"

No one can say that the New Age Movement does not embrace and incorporate every strange thing that's out there. There are literally thousands of eclectic New Age groups around the world; no one knows exactly how many. They represent people in the media, in science, medicine, business, schools, hospitals, and in high levels of governments. They influence everything from politics, to science, to ecology, to education. They have infiltrated the mainstream of our culture. Sometimes, they are easily recognizable, and other times, they are well hidden. They insist that they learn through experience and that they gain knowledge by learning a technique and applying it. However, it is the subliminal message of a force being responsible for their well-being, rather than God, that is so dangerous

OPRAH

To bring this all into perspective, a more contemporary example is in order. So it's time to fearlessly move ahead with someone whose sphere of influence knows no bounds, whose main claim to fame is her notoriety, and who is known immediately upon uttering a first name: Oprah.

A rags to riches story if ever there was one. A genuinely kind and giving person who crashed through every barrier, when some said that no woman could do it—particularly no black woman. She has become an "expert" in many fields, and her followers number in the millions. If she promotes you, your book, or your movie, you can take it to the bank that it will be a raging success. She truly has the Midas touch and a sensitivity that eludes most of us mere mortals. There is not a topic she will not tackle with energy and a spirit of wanting to help. This is fine—even welcomed—when she is touting a new product, diet, or even a health remedy, but when she steps into the God arena, she has some very large shoes to fill.

Unfortunately, too many people are not selective enough when it comes to leaders like Oprah Winfrey. Following her sage-sounding, heartfelt advice can lead you to a place that is fraught with New Age ideas and philosophies. Her vast media empire and limitless reach provide a platform for her ideologies. Most are subtle mixtures of her early Mississippi, poverty-stricken, Baptist, Christian upbringing, generously sprinkled with a rather large portion of New Age spirituality. Some of her recent handpicked protégés seem to pull together bits and pieces of many diverse philosophies, and the final product morphs into their version of the truth.

OPRAH'S BELIEFS

Oprah puts much time and her considerable resources behind those projects in which she believes. The problem is that more and more of those she endorses are "spiritual teachers" whose sweet-sounding messages trample the very basics of Christianity. While it seems that Oprah truly believes that there is no corruption or contradiction in joining these philosophies, this really drives home the point of just how cunning and deceitful the New Age religion is.

"In the program Oprah revealed she didn't think God is hung up on what you believe about God—whatever that "force" is, it doesn't care what you call it. He doesn't have an ego problem. She states, 'I believe in the *force*—I call it God.' She also said if you believe in the rhythm of nature and in love, then you believe in God" (Watchman Fellowship 1998, 2).

Some of Oprah's projects include her ten-week "webinar" with self-proclaimed spiritual teacher Eckhart Tolle. This joint effort is based on Tolle's book, *A New Earth*. He has said on this ten-week interactive webinar, he takes practices from Buddhism, Islam, and Christianity and presents them in a "live in the present" format—find your "higher self" by distancing yourself from your ego. In speaking of what we call God, whether it be Buddha or Krisna or Allah, Tolle said, "Don't get attached to any one word. You can substitute 'Christ' for presence, if that is more meaningful to you. Christ is your God-essence of the Self, as it is sometimes called in the East..." (Tolle 1999, 104).

A WIDE AUDIENCE

Oprah also offered daily classes on XM Satellite Radio, on the book—*A Course in Miracles*—that once again had a very Christian-sounding title. Unfortunately, though, this book was supposedly dictated by an inner voice, which the author, Marianne Williamson, attributes to Jesus Christ, but there are things in it that clearly contradict the Bible and the teachings of Jesus. For example, according to the book and teaching, there is no such thing as sin.

Oprah has been on this track for a while now. A few years ago, she helped to create "The Secret" phenomenon that swept through the country. Positive thinking, while a good thing, is not what propels people to their dream endings. While the Bible teaches that thoughts can be powerful, it is only so when your thoughts line up with God's thoughts. You are not the Creator; He is. It is a shame that a person like Oprah, with such a high profile, has chosen to take this course.

The New Age speak, this feel-good stuff, which always comes back to you having total control and becoming a little god for yourself, is just subtle and sly enough to sound good and draw people—even Christians—away from core beliefs. This country has already embraced the New Age with open arms; we don't need advice and direction on spiritual matters from a celebrity, no matter how sweet, popular, open, and giving she is. Our daily lives should be guided by the Manufacturer's handbook—the Bible. You would not go to a Volkswagen dealer to fix your Porsche. Why would you go to your radio, TV, magazine, or even the latest guru to find the meaning of life?

NEW AGE AND THE BIBLE

Christians, at least, need to wake up and be aware of this evil force that is snowballing right under our noses. We should be prepared and aware that we are living in the last days. Evil will grow, and it will even look like it will win, but it won't! However, there will be some spiritual battles as well as natural ones.

"But in his estate shall he honour the God of forces: and a god whom his fathers knew not shall he honour..." (Daniel 11:38, KJV).

This prophecy concerning the antichrist speaks directly to his chosen religion. The "god of forces" is definitely who the New Agers call their god—"more of a force than a being." Of course, this would be a god unfamiliar to the people of Daniel's day, one they did not know.

The Bible forecasts a time of great rebellion against God, when one world ruler would exalt himself as the one and only true god. The pieces are coming together as the New Age leaders have set the stage, putting into motion all that is necessary for One-World Government and religion that their hero can rule and reign over.

Their agenda and implementation of it have confounded most of those who try to penetrate their confusing and often contradictory religion. Along with their "Christ" there is an evolution where man can become god. This convoluted process and theory have made many back away, and through the following quote by Alice Bailey, we can see that the confusion is intentional.

"These ancient Mysteries (concerning the man-god process) were originally given to humanity by the Hierarchy and contain the entire clue to the evolutionary process, *hidden* in numbers, in ritual, in words and in symbology; these *veil* secret of man's origin and destiny they provide also the teaching which humanity needs in order to pass from darkness to Light, from the unreal to the real and from death to Immortality" (Bailey 1948, 121–122).

A REPLAY

Christians as well as Jews become targets for persecution during this time of rebellion (Matthew 24:9). Every religion on this planet is coming together as part of the New Age—all the Eastern religions (except perhaps Islam), and Christian cults. All these philosophies and religions together are embraced by the New Age, from mantra to karma to reincarnation, from yoga to gurus, and to Tibetan deities.

Astrology, tarot reading, séances, channeling, crystals, and transcendental meditation are the integral parts. Evolution, ecology, holistic medicine, and extremists of every group imaginable are all included and welcomed as part of this great movement, which is already underway. The "Age of Aquarius" is based in astrology, which in turn is based on witchcraft.

The modern start to this philosophy and religion may have been at the time of Hitler, but the practices and ideas they embrace come from a much more ancient time. You would think that, with all the centuries that have passed, we would have somehow seen through these satanic practices. Yet, with a little twist here and a little tweak there, we are back in the unsophisticated times of paganism—the ancient days of sun worship and witchcraft. What's amazing is that no one is the wiser.

There was a series of movies entitled *Back to the Future,* and that's what it seems like when one is speaking of centuries-old beliefs like paganism. Yet, that is where New Age is taking us, and we're buying it! The goal is to get people to believe in the revolving door they call reincarnation—changing people until they reach that spiritual nirvana and identify the god within.

NO NEW TRICKS

Since the beginning of time, Satan's plan has been to try to get man to believe that he could become as God. It was in the garden of Eden when Satan, aptly disguised as a serpent, appeared to Eve.

> And he said to the woman, "Has God indeed said, 'You shall not eat of every tree of the garden'?" And the woman said to the serpent, "We may eat of the fruit of the trees of the garden;

but of the fruit of the tree which is in the midst of the garden, God has said, 'You shall not eat it, nor shall you touch it, lest you die.'" Then the serpent said to the woman, "You will not surely die. For God knows that in the day you eat of it your eyes will be opened, and you will be like God ...

Genesis 3:1b–5

Here we are, thousands of years later, and Satan is telling the same lie. He knows this lie well; it is the reason he was thrown out of heaven. He thought he could be as God. Yet, no matter how trite the lie, somehow we always fall for it. Perhaps there is something in us that seeks power and control, and Satan knows it. Be that as it may, the fact is that the New Age Movement has as a central doctrine this same principle of evolving through reincarnation to become as God.

Also, in that same exchange, Satan says to Eve, "You will not surely die." This is a second tenet of the New Age religion, which speaks to the immortality of the soul. Of course, this plays right into the minds of humans who would just rather not think of ever dying or of ever being held accountable for anything. Through this process of reincarnation, which eventually helps us reach our god state, we can also avoid death and or accountability.

CHRISTIANITY VERSUS NEW AGE

New Agers believe that humans are divine and are capable of creating their own reality. Christians know there is but one God. "I am the Lord, and there is no other; there is no God besides me. I will gird you, though you have not known Me, that they may know from the rising of the sun to its setting, that there is none beside Me. I am the Lord and there is no other;" (Isaiah 45:5–6).

New Agers believe that the basic flaw in mankind is that humans don't know they are divine. The Bible tells us that man's basic problem is sin, "for all have sinned and fall short of the glory of God" (Romans 3:23). "If we say that we have no sin, we deceive ourselves, and the truth is not in us" (1 John 1:8).

All is one, and all is God—pantheism—is what New Agers believe. Romans 1:25 says, "Who exchanged the truth of God for the lie, and worshiped and served the creature rather than the Creator …" God and His creation are separate, and God is far above that which He created—us.

New Agers, like Buddhists—remember Lucifer said that Buddha was one of the names you could call him—seek enlightenment. As they travel through various lives, practicing mind techniques like meditation and visualization, they come closer to what Buddha termed nirvana and what New Agers call divinity.

Christians, however, seek salvation. They realize that the answer is not within themselves and that they cannot save themselves. They realize that Jesus the Christ came, and through His death and resurrection, offered us the free gift of salvation.

"For He made Him who knew no sin to be sin for us, that we might become the righteousness of God in Him" (2 Corinthians 5:21).

There are many other differences between Christianity and New Age, too numerous to mention. They hold opposite views in every doctrine. New Agers have perverted Jesus—who He is and what He stands for. Their blasphemy will know no bounds in the not-too-distant future. They are no longer hiding in closets; their agenda is right out in the open for anyone to see. Meanwhile, our secular, liberal media, with their denigration of anything Christian, has unwittingly helped their cause immensely.

THE AQUARIAN CONSPIRACY

Once more, you can be assured that these people are not kidding, and this truly is nothing new. It has been masterfully disguised and woven throughout the decades. In 1980 Marilyn Ferguson wrote a book called *The Aquarian Conspiracy*, which reveals the extent of the New Age Movement.

It acknowledges New Age being a huge organization with representatives everywhere, including the cabinet of the president of the U.S. at that time. She calls it "a powerful network, a new mind—the ascendance of a startling world view."

She tells how the organization stays large, strong, and viable. She claims it is put together in a most unique fashion, like "a badly-knotted fishnet." This type of organization—or non-organization, if you will—allows for each group, chapter, or whatever to work independently of the next. Should there be a problem in one cell, it would not affect the others. It cannot be sabotaged from within, and it would be nearly impossible to bring it all down at once, except, of course, that God has a plan.

Actually, it is pretty ingenious, putting together a religion/political/social movement that seems disorganized and non-threatening—even fanciful—to any outsider and to all but a few insiders. It has so many subplots and interests that untangling it would take a lifetime. It has a mystical language and an almost crazy mission that surely no one would believe is diabolical.

To have it so accepted by intelligent people is amazing, but the New Age Movement is all these things and more. It could very well be Satan's vehicle for ushering in the antichrist. The Bible says he will be a charismatic, influential man—one who seems kind and generous at first, who will be one who believes strongly in this philosophy/religion that will give him the world.

A SUMMARY

While it might seem as though this group is disorganized and even fanatical, they are very crafty. They have been amazingly successful. Their subtlety and deceit emanate from their leadership and filter down. The lower echelon of their groups is often kept in the dark with the same song of peace, love, and tolerance from the sixties and seventies.

Each New Age group is different. Some groups stress more of one thing than the other. There is little cohesion. The more confusion the better for the leaders of this occult movement. Yet there is a camaraderie and agreement among its followers. It's doubtful that many of the average people who call themselves New Agers would admit or even be aware that it is occult in nature. Some may even call themselves Christian. New Agers embrace every form of mysticism—the occult, Eastern philosophies, astrology, etc. This includes the same anti-Semitic ideals of Hitler, as well as Social Darwinism. Evolution and fanatical ecology are just other banners they rally around. Their interests are wide and varied, and once again, that is no accident.

Speaking of Darwin, one cannot overemphasize the importance of Darwin's "survival of the fittest" concept to a successful future of the New Age. This is why, despite all the evidence to the contrary, we are still teaching Darwin's outdated, unproven *theory* over 150 years after it was written. Social Darwinism is the logical outgrowth of evolution. It is being spoon-fed to our children and integrated into their curricula. This wraps it all into one neat package—evolution, Social Darwinism, neo-Nazism, and the New Age.

MARCIA'S STORY

There is a woman who knows firsthand about New Age and the occult. She can tell you how real it is and how pervasive it is becoming. Marcia grew up in an alcoholic home and moved around a lot. As a child, she was both curious and religious. She became a high school loner, and in college, her search for some deeper meaning to life led her to begin to experiment with the paranormal.

Marcia wanted something more experiential, more real than what Christianity had to offer; she wanted answers to life's great mysteries. She continued her search. She visited psychics and astrologers regularly. She read many books, attended consciousness classes, and made friends with those involved in these phenomena. Marcia jumped into the occult and Eastern philosophies with both feet and was eventually introduced to her "spiritual master."

Marcia's attitude of anger and defiance, cultivated since childhood, helped her to delve deeper into the paranormal without fear. She had out-of-body experiences and had contact with spiritual entities. She learned to visualize, meditate, chant, do psychic healings, and more. Reincarnation and other Eastern philosophies seemed to answer her questions about the hereafter.

Marcia took a seven-hour exam in astrology, which she passed to get her license. Eventually, she taught astrology and wrote for New Age journals. Her experiences took her to the dark recesses of the paranormal. Marcia had frightening encounters with the spirit world. She learned the consummate basis for New Ageism—relativism, with no absolutes and no truth except what one experiences. As Marcia's quest for something deeper materialized, so did the feeling that the answers she was getting were not answers; her experiments with the occult simply posed more questions.

THE TRUTH WILL SET YOU FREE

As Marcia began to question the nonsensical aspect of New Age—no one truth, no one answer, no one reality—she had a strange but strong compulsion to go to church. After going through a gamut of emotions, including anger, Marcia finally gave in. She even reasoned that perhaps this one visit would put her in touch with a former life as a priest. During that first service, Marcia experienced the love of God "wash over and through" her.

That was the beginning for Marcia. Within weeks, she began to know Jesus through His Word—the Bible—and was reading it when she got saved. She soon learned of His realness and His love. Since that day, she has stayed with God and learned much. Marcia says that the greatest difference in her life today, as a Christian, is that she is spiritually satisfied. Once the void inside us is filled by God, it is what completes us, guides us, and gives us inner peace.

This is a true story of a woman who could have been the poster child for the occult, who has come back from a dark hole called New Age. Today, Marcia has her own ministry called CANA—Christian Answers for the New Age—which informs and educates about the New Age occult beliefs. She responds to those involved with the truth of Christ. CANA is an excellent and needed resource, especially for the time of deception in which we live.

IT IS HAPPENING

When we erase all moral and spiritual boundaries and make it trendy to get involved with the metaphysical, when group-think and karma become the tools of the masses, and an entire generation grows up with it:

What happens is the inevitable, out of chaos and apathy (the destruction of the old order) rises a mass movement (a new order). It feeds on the loss of individual thinking, but in return promises a secure, responsibility-free place in the Group Mind where thinking is done for you. It removes all rights to family autonomy, but guarantees a lifelong brotherhood; outlaws all religions except its own, but provides ego-friendly answers for all life's questions. It requires you to die but offers a Supreme Opportunity to give up your life with honor and dignity, and a sense of intrinsic value as a tiny cog in the Vast Plan. It's better than being lost and lonely. And after all, there is no real death, nor is there any particular reason to hang onto this life; why not pay the karma sooner than later?

(Hannah Newman, *The Rainbow Swastika*, under "Nazism and New Age")

WRAP UP

The New Age Movement has, to some extent, seeped into every aspect of life in most countries around the world. Everything about it is nebulous. It goes by many names; it embraces many tenets; it uses Celtic, occult, and pagan terms; and it encompasses witchcraft, mysticism, Satan worship, and many other religions and practices. It welcomes tarot cards, séances, channelers, crystals, astrology, metaphysics, and conjurers.

New Age has infiltrated every human endeavor, whether political, religious, societal, educational, or organizational.

The poison that has slowly, deceptively crept into the everyday lives of everyday people has also been a factor in various government and quasi-government organizations, where much greater damage can be done. We Christians have all wondered at one time or another, "How could Adam and Eve be so easily deceived?" or "How come the Jews didn't recognize their own Messiah?" There were so many prophecies made, and He fulfilled them all! "Why didn't more people get into the ark?" All these things seem simple to us in retrospect. I'm certain the New Age and its helpers will be that obvious too, one day—soon!

CHAPTER THREE:

VEHICLES OF THE ANTICHRIST

A UNITED EUROPE,
THE NEW ROMAN EMPIRE—

THE UN—A PUPPET,
STRINGS PULLED BY A LIAR!

There are areas where the New Age Movement has a strong foothold, but because of its ability to be a chameleon, most are unaware of its presence. For example, the European Union (EU) has already been influenced by the New Age philosophy/ religion. New Agers see national boundaries in a different way than most of us, usually as temporary. They see their goals, such as a greater emphasis on environment, as being accomplished in stages. First, on the regional level in organizations such as the EU and then later fully expanded planet-wide through New World Order (NWO) agenda and the United Nations.

The EU is a logical extension of their plan for a New World Order. Those involved think that world peace can only be achieved through the implementation of One-World Government. This would accomplish a cessation of warring nation-states whose natural conflicts of interest inevitably lead to wars that suck other nations into their vortex. Of course, part of this plan for a New World Order includes a worldwide religion, one world monetary system, one world police state, and eventually, a worldwide government with one great ruler.

NWO AGENDA

It should be noted that many consider the NWO to be a monstrous conspiracy to defuse the sovereignty of larger countries, such as the U.S., and to destroy the power of established institutions like organized religion in general and Christianity in particular. Regardless of the validity of such thinking, there is no doubt that, at the very least, an agenda named the NWO now exists, and that it has as one of its purposes One-World Government.

The evidence of the importance of this agenda is outlined by the statement President H.W. Bush made on January 16, 1991, in an oval office speech, "If we do not follow the dictates of our inner moral compass–lawlessness will threaten the peace–and the emerging New World Order we now see" (Bush 1991, 1A). Many other leaders have joined in with President Bush's philosophy. Pope John Paul II stated, "One-World Government is inevitable" (Martin 1990, 124).

Joe Biden, then senator, had an article in the *Wall Street Journal* entitled, "How I learned to love the New World Order" (Biden 1992, A13). You may say, "Well, that was twenty years ago". Fourteen years later President Obama (then senator) in his book *Audacity of Hope* wrote, "When the world's sole super power willingly restrains its power and abides by internationally agreed-upon standards of conduct it sends a message" (Obama 2006, 159). President Obama has made his stance for a New World Order very obvious. In both his speeches and his inferences, his position is quite clear. For example, in an article in the *Washington Times* in 2009, *Times* journalist Jeffery T. Kuhner accuses Obama of creating a New World Order through his environmental policies. He quotes Christopher Moncton, a major advisor to former British Prime Minister Margaret Thatcher, as saying, "President Obama is on a path toward establishing a one-world government" (Kuhner 2009, 1)

So while there may not yet be a structured organization called the NWO, it certainly exists in the minds and plans of many great leaders. This has been a desire burning in the hearts of many, Americans and others, for a long time. And now everything seems to be moving in that direction. It is obvious that such thinkers would find the EU, wherein the national members have already surrendered some of their sovereignty, to be on the right track. Moreover, the European Union might be linked with other similar organizations such as the Trilateral Commission.

THE EUROPEAN UNION

While New Agers are opposed to some multinational organizations such as large corporations, they see others as being helpful to them. Thus, New Agers and the EU will most likely peacefully coexist and probably promote each other. As the New Age philosophy/religion is growing in Europe, as it is worldwide, this would outwardly appear to be a plus for the further growth and success of the EU.

Aside from the impact of the New World Order and the New Agers, the EU may have had some help from the spiritual side of things. Turning to the Bible's descriptions of end-times events, there should be a pathway for a national leader to become a worldwide leader. For the antichrist to carry out the predictions made for him, he must be in charge of some type of worldwide organization, and this will require some fairly immediate changes in the power of such organizations.

In the end-times scenario, it would appear that the antichrist assumes various levels of political power over time. But he will rely more on this political power than on his military strength, at least most of the time. The Bible does indicate that he will encounter opposition from three nations that could be military in nature. A logical route to political power over time would be to achieve the presidency of a major EU Member State, then assume control over the EU, and eventually move to political control of the world.

Thus, spiritual powers from both sides, working in concert to achieve the same end but for different purposes, may aid in the overall success of the EU. It becomes a convenient vehicle to carry the coming son of Satan to world dominance. Certainly, the EU has been more of a success than many expected. They have a total of twenty-seven member nations and their own currency, the Euro, used exclusively in most of the Member States. Be that as it may, first we need to know how this European powerhouse came together.

FROM HUMBLE BEGINNINGS

The European Union was formed based upon the laudable assumption that if Europeans would stop killing and maiming each other in search of a united Europe, this would be a good thing. Of course, those who desired a united Europe through-out time often were not interested in this for altruistic reasons. Instead, they wished to have the power and wealth of the emperors of the Roman Empire, which fell in AD 476. Thus, the name Holy Roman Empire was devised in 962 to try to bring back the grandeur, wealth, and power of the original Roman Empire at its zenith in AD 117. Like many imitations, this fabrication between the Germanic kings and the Pope, which lasted for almost a thousand years, failed to come even close to matching the original Roman Empire.

There is no method of calculating the carnage of the distant past. There is no way anyone can know for sure what previous centuries have contributed, in terms of bloodshed, since the fall of the Roman Empire. However, in the pursuit of European unity of the twentieth century alone, there was a loss of life of an estimated 63 million persons. Apparently, when putting aside greed and covetousness and considering all parties' needs, a successful union can be achieved. It can only be viewed as bitterly ironic that the successful European Union of the twenty-first century was initially formed in the mid-twentieth century without a single shot being fired.

HOW IT CAME TOGETHER

The roots of the European Union can be traced back to 1950, when it was decided that the binding together of France and Germany, on an economic basis, would eliminate much of the friction between them. The agreement was joined by Italy, the Netherlands, Belgium, and Luxembourg. These six nations formed the European Coal and Steel Community.

In 1951, the six countries (the ECSC) started operating as the first united European community. The idea was that they were not going to attack their neighbors if they were business partners. There were also other practical benefits that came out of this arrangement.

The Treaty of Rome was ratified in 1957, and it allowed for the abolishment of customs duties among the six nations. Trade both within and outside of the six-nation bloc, now named the European Economic Community (EEC), skyrocketed. In 1963, the six nations signed agreements with their former colonies to reduce trade restrictions and tariffs. This caused an increase in trade with Asia, Africa, and the Caribbean.

In 1973, Denmark, Ireland, and the United Kingdom became members. In the eighties, Greece, Spain, and Portugal joined. In 1979, the European Parliament, which has powers of control over the executive branch, switched from an appointed body to one where direct elections by the people of Europe determine the membership. Parliament also shares budgetary power with the executive branch.

In 1986, the Single European Act was instituted. The purpose of this act was to eliminate all restrictions among those member nations. In 1993, the Treaty on European Union was signed. The EU was now a fully functioning government with a Commission (executive branch), Parliament, and Court of Justice. Member states had to hand over some of their sovereignty in areas such as foreign and security policy, immigration, and police and justice. The stated purpose for this was greater efficiency in commerce and more effectiveness in fighting organized crime and drug trafficking.

UNIFIED MONETARY SYSTEM

Perhaps most importantly, it was decided to go ahead with monetary union, and the new currency—the Euro—is now in use. Fifteen of the total nations had joined the Euro bloc by early 2010. The United Kingdom was the only major nation holdout. The strong Euro is usually competing well with the other international currencies, including the U.S. dollar. Clearly, the Euro is proof to all that the EU is not only here to stay but can and will be a major player on the world economic scene. This puts us one step closer to the one world monetary system that the Bible calls for and the antichrist must have during end times. It is also a goal of the New Age Movement.

It should be noted that most member nations, with three exceptions, have committed to changing over to the Euro once they have fulfilled the requirements to do so. The exceptions are the United Kingdom, Denmark, and Sweden, which have special opt-outs. Even the United Kingdom may eventually have to convert to the Euro or risk losing out on trade opportunities. The EU is the largest exporter in the world and the second-largest importer. Trading with the pound against the Euro means that Anglo-European traders have to assume currency fluctuation risk—a risk that doesn't exist if the UK goes to the Euro.

There is no denying that not only is the twenty-seven Member State EU in place, but it is functioning efficiently, and its future appears bright despite the recent recession impacting many EU nations. Official candidate countries for new membership keeps growing. The expansion of the European Union is inevitable with the possibilities of it eventually encompassing most of Europe and even parts of Asia.

VARIOUS FUNCTIONS AND INFRASTRUCTURE

Elected every five years by popular vote, the European Parliament represents a population that is approaching 500 million persons—well above that of the U.S. The European Union has the second-largest Gross Domestic Product in the world. The Parliament shares with the Council the power to legislate and appropriate funds and exercises supervision over the Commission.

The Council is the EU's main decision-making body. It adopts measures in the fields of police and judicial cooperation in interstate criminal matters. The Commission presents legislative proposals to Parliament and the Council. It functions as the EU's executive body and represents the Union in international matters, mostly trade. The Court of Justice ensures that EU law is uniformly interpreted. The European Central Bank implements European monetary policy. The Presidency, as of now, is held on a six-month, rotating basis by the head of state of each of the member nations. The role of this office is to represent the European Union in international organizations and in other EU institutions and to enhance cooperation between member countries.

There is not yet a unified EU military force. Right now, the EU has what is called European Union Battlegroups, numbering fifteen, with 1,500 soldiers per group. The EU has deployed troops in peacekeeping missions in Africa and other areas.

THE TIME IS RIGHT

The current organization of the EU is already perfect for takeover by a charismatic leader of one of the Member States. This person could legitimately wait his turn to assume the presidency, then, at the end of his term, simply refuse to step down. Of course, there would be much preparation behind the scenes to ensure the success of such a brazen move.

A crisis, real or imagined, could precipitate this, and the loyalty of the EU army (when it comes into being), plus the president's own state army, could ensure such a coup. This would be a lot easier than trying to conquer Europe by force. Needless to say, this could be best accomplished by a large and powerful Member State.

A threatening development, such as a war in the Middle East, could easily provide the impetus for a bloodless coup. In times of stress, many would simply like to turn over their affairs to a strong leader. It is important to remember that the member nations will have already turned most, if not all, of their sovereignty to the EU. Bear in mind the Court of Justice already supersedes national law in many areas. Also, all European members are subject to the actions of the European Central Bank. It wouldn't be a great stretch to give up a little more national power, especially if there seems to be a good reason for it.

A REUNITED EUROPE

The growth and development of the European Union is truly one of the remarkable events of the past sixty years. For centuries, the dream of a reunited Europe had eluded everyone who tackled the problem, whether from a military or a political point of view.

Each attempt to unite the nations only seemed to prove that once Europe was broken, it couldn't be put back together on a permanent basis again. The frustration of this task is embodied in the nursery rhyme about Humpty Dumpty—all the king's horses and all the king's men couldn't put Humpty together again.

While some of these efforts included the role of the powerful Catholic Church, it still did not matter. After a short span of cohesiveness, the leader of the day died or fell from power, and the Empire, fleetingly seen, was gone again. Charlemagne, the Holy Roman Emperors, Napoleon, Bismarck, and Hitler all had their brief moment in the sun, but it was all over almost as soon as it began. The Third Reich was supposed to last one thousand years but only was in power for twelve. Hitler's invasions of his peaceful neighbors gave him temporary control over most of continental Europe, but only for a brief two years.

CREDIT MONNET

It was left for the Frenchman, Jean Monnet, to see the true problem and to solve it with a most cunning proposal. Throughout much of European history, the neighbors of France and Germany found themselves in competition for the position of the leader of Europe. Like two neighborhood bullies, they just had to fight each other.

Monnet solved that issue by suggesting to Germany an economic partnership. Monnet reasoned that business partners may not necessarily like each other, but they would not fight each other if it was not in their own best interests. Linking the two countries together economically could definitely solve that problem.

Monnet's true genius lay in his understanding of the power of the outgrowths of his idea. He believed that such an economic partnership could lead to the reduction of tariffs and other trade restrictions, and this would increase trade and speed up economic growth. Also, he thought, it was quite possible that if he were correct, other nations would want to join the coalition. If fact, it might be that the other nations of Western Europe would almost be forced to join the new entity. The strength and clarity of his vision were such that the initial effort was in fact joined by four other countries.

A GREAT VISION

Of course, the fall of the Soviet Union and the Berlin Wall opened up the possibility that the EU could be enlarged to include Central and Eastern Europe—a fact that Monnet could not have possibly foreseen in the early fifties. Now that a number of these nations have applied for or have become members, it appears that the final size of the EU will be only as limited as its Member States wish to make it.

At the present time, it is clearly the second richest, largest trading bloc, and its main competitor on the world scene, NAFTA, will probably always be smaller in terms of Member States (Mexico, the U.S., and Canada) despite the size and wealth of the U.S. One indication of the success of the EU is the viability of the Euro.

The fact that all this was done peacefully also reflects well on Monnet's vision. After a long and successful career, he became one of the first Europeans to receive the U.S. Presidential Medal of Freedom. He is frequently referred to as the architect of United Europe or the father of the EU. It is interesting to note that he was born one year earlier than Adolf Hitler, in 1888, in Cognac, France. It is strange, indeed, that two contemporary men with the same idea of reuniting Europe could have taken such different paths. Jean Monnet was a true visionary, while Hitler was a demagogue.

A LEVEL PLAYING FIELD

For all its success, a major part of the united Europe dream remains unfulfilled. Many Europeans view the EU as a haven for overzealous Eurocrats and lawyers. To some extent this is true, as much of the initial work involved tedious labor concerning trade restrictions and the like. Monnet's dream, however, was that not only would the states unite for economic reasons, but a complete union would bring about a true United States of Europe.

Up until now, it must be said that some of the old nationalism is very much evident. A Frenchman still considers himself to be a Frenchman first and a European second. Monnet stated in a 1952 speech that, "We are not building a coalition between states, but a union among people." This has not occured yet.

What the EU does well is provide a relatively level playing field for its Member States and the EU as a whole. The European Union is not afraid to take on rich, multinational corporations who would like to exploit any weaknesses they see in the European market. For example, the EU accused Microsoft of illegally tying its media player into its Windows operating system and withholding key information from rivals to try to win more of the market for computer servers. Microsoft has successfully fought against antitrust laws in the U.S., but the EU has pursued antitrust action for several years and refused to back down to the software giant. In 2008, the EU levied a $1.4 million fine against Microsoft for failing to live up to its antitrust agreements with the EU.

THE EUROPEAN UNION

While the EU continues to grow, it is interesting to speculate on some of the forces that influenced Monnet. He was known primarily as a diplomat who was recognized as an authority at settling multilateral disputes between nations. There is no question that he hoped his vision for Europe would be realized and that it included a political union of all of the nations of Europe or, at the time, Western Europe. While this has not yet been accomplished, there seems to be no reason to doubt that it will. Such a political union would make it even easier for a Member State leader to assume the leadership of Europe, perhaps even by legal and peaceful means.

It is important to realize that the EU is not a state and thus does not have its own dedicated military forces. An early attempt to do this in 1952 failed, and there have been no serious attempts since then. However, there are armies on paper that are made up of Member States' armed forces. In addition, small peacekeeping missions have been carried out. A peacekeeping mission to supervise the 2006 Congolese elections was viewed as a success, but a report on the mission revealed tensions between the joint French-German forces, and the German forces were not allowed by their government to enter dangerous areas. While it is not surprising that French and German troops might not get along too well, this seems to have been a mission that succeeded in spite of itself.

GERMANY CALLING THE SHOTS

On March 23, 2007—on the occasion of the EU's fiftieth birthday—German Chancellor Angela Merkel, who was the EU President at that time, expressed her wish for a unified

European Army. While the timing was not right, it is clear that some of the leaders of the EU would like their own large, dedicated fighting force.

The Treaty of Lisbon took effect on December 1, 2009, and revised some internal EU procedures. This treaty was a compromise to replace the proposed new EU constitution, which failed in 2005. The new treaty appears to give the EU more power over its states in certain areas and contains a reference to the establishment of a mutual defense force.

This was reinforced on February 8, 2010, when German Foreign Minister Guido Westerwelle again called for plans for a European army. He said that an EU army is part of being a "global player." Germany received backing from Russia, who is not a member of the EU. Perhaps their thinking was that if an EU army was established it would presumably replace NATO, which is a stronger force. The idea that the presence of the U.S. would no longer be a factor in Europe would open up possibilities to Russia to regain control over some of the smaller Eastern European countries, such as they did with part of Georgia in 2009.

While Hitler hoped that the major Axis powers (Germany, Italy, and Japan) would rule the world at the end of World War II, he would have been quite happy with his leadership role as the dictator of a united Europe. This will not be the case for the antichrist, and thus, the EU should only be viewed as a stepping-stone to world political and military power. To accomplish this will require the use of a greater vehicle, one that would give him access beyond the continent of Europe. He would need a platform from which to hypnotize the world, weaken world powers, deplete powerhouse armies, and promise true world peace.

No, the United States of Europe would simply not be enough for the son of Satan, nor would it be enough for the New Age plan. A worldwide religion demands a One-World Government, which to Americans—snug as can be in our little corner of the world—seems impossible. However, the truth is that it will not take decades to institute such a platform; it won't even take years. It already exists right on our soil. It is the United Nations.

THE UN AND ITS COMPONENTS

The United Nations was established in 1945, almost immediately after the cessation of hostilities in World War II. This brand-new international organization loomed large on the tiny island of Manhattan. As a young, innocent ten-year-old girl getting off the school bus, I was not as impressed as the other children in my fifth-grade class seemed to be. After all, I was born and raised in New York. My family had moved to New Jersey only in the last year or so; no, I was not wide-eyed and could contain myself about the tall buildings, bustling crowds, and honking horns—at least at first.

Once we entered the building, everything seemed to change! There was an aura about this place that was built on U.S. soil in the heart of New York City but was not part of New York or even the United States. Of course, it was the United Nations building, and we were escorted from chamber to chamber. I soon was under the spell of this bigger-than-life edifice. In fact, to my ten-year-old mind, I decided my future right then and there. I had just taken off the earphones that were used to translate the speaker into various languages, and I had an epiphany. I was going to be an interpreter for the UN—an English-to-French interpreter.

I had that dream for quite some time. I even managed to squeeze five years of French into my four years of high school. I have come a long way from that time of my fifth-grade school trip, but the United Nations always held a special place in my heart. That is why when I began researching for this book, I thought it would be like revisiting an old friend, but nothing could be further from the truth.

The UN is, and always has been, dedicated to the New Age agenda. They are absolutely sold out to the idea of a New World Order and a global economy. They are more than willing to crush the individual for the good of the group, but I'm getting ahead of things here. First, it is necessary to know the structure and purpose of this international organization.

A PEACEKEEPING FORCE

The two main, stated goals of the UN are to prevent wars and to maintain and establish human dignity, though many now suspect more sinister goals—for instance, the goal of One-World Government, which the UN would preside over. The record of the UN to date has been spotty. There have been no world wars since the UN was founded, but whether this was as a result of the UN's efforts or a natural reluctance on the part of most nations to engage in something that could lead to a nuclear catastrophe is far from clear.

Certainly, the UN has been helpful in areas such as Korea and more recently as a peacekeeper in the former Yugoslavia. The UN has also had peacekeeping operations in Africa, which has been torn by ethnic violence and civil wars.

It would be accurate to say that the UN has been most effective as a peacekeeping force once peace has been established. The United Nations forces, trained in a peacekeeping role, are usually much more appropriate and useful than the typical military force when occupation to maintain the peace becomes the objective. In other areas, the UN has been far less proficient.

There are a number of reasons for this. Most notably, the UN is made up of virtually all nations of the world—192 in all, counting the addition of the former Yugoslav state of Montenegro in 2006. For even a majority of them to agree on a single course of action is an extremely unlikely event. Under these circumstances, the UN becomes a large debating society in which each nation has an opportunity to present its own agenda and the rationale for it.

UN WEAKNESSES

Part of the UN's weakness in many situations can be attributed to its structure and the method of financing its operations. The United Nations headquarters are in New York City, and the site is made up of several buildings reflecting some of the different functions within the structure. The immediate area surrounding the headquarters and the headquarters themselves are in international territory.

The General Assembly is that part of the UN where all members are represented. The charter permits the Assembly to discuss any question of importance to the UN and to recommend action to be taken by the members or by other departments within the UN.

The Security Council has the major responsibility in the UN for keeping the peace. The Council has five permanent and ten rotating members. The five permanent members are France, Great Britain, China, Russia, and the United States. The other ten members are elected to two-year terms by the General Assembly. This is the most powerful of the UN groups, in that it has the authority to decide what action the UN should take to settle international disputes.

A major problem for the UN is that the Security Council can act only if nine members, including all five permanent members, agree to do so. A "no" vote by any of the five permanent members defeats the proposal despite how many others vote for it. It is not difficult to see how one of these five nations could easily be opposed to just about any proposal set before the Security Council. Russia, in particular, has a history of being "veto-happy".

The U.S. has tried to be more judicious in their use of the veto, leading many UN critics to complain that we are giving up part of our sovereignty to the United Nations while getting nothing out of it except headaches and the largest membership dues bill. The UN refused to back the U.S. in toppling Saddam Hussein in Iraq, but several months later wanted the U.S. to send troops to Liberia, where a civil war was raging.

OTHER PROBLEMS

There is a whole host of problems that an effective UN could deal with that have nothing to do with wars. These include, but are not limited to, peaceful uses for outer space, the seabed and Antarctica, world hunger, international aviation, atomic energy, human rights, and the like. The problems that plague the UN in seeking the peace also hamper it in these areas.

Two examples indicate the futility of working within the UN structure. After the Gulf War, Saddam Hussein, leader of Iraq, agreed that he would allow certain actions to be taken by the UN. One of these was to allow UN inspectors to freely enter his country to verify that there were no weapons of mass destruction there. As

Saddam had used poison gas on his own people and against the Iranians in a war in the eighties, it was clear he had no scruples in this area. He refused to cooperate. Finally, tired of trying to get the UN to act in this obvious area of responsibility, the U.S. and Great Britain took matters into their own hands, and they were aided by a few other nations, notably Australia, Canada, and Poland.

The second example is Iran's nuclear arms program. While the UN pontificated and threatened, Iran kept moving ahead aided by outside forces. As a member of the Security Council, China, which has a close relationship with Iran (and needs its oil), always has the ability to block any UN sanctions. Therefore, any action against Iran will probably come from a willing coalition of nations outside of the UN. Iran with nuclear weapons is like giving a child dynamite and a match; it's only a matter of time before disaster strikes.

SHORTCOMINGS AND FAILURES

Then there is the deplorable matter of human rights. This is an area which the UN could concentrate on with the certain knowledge that only the offenders could possibly be opposed to their actions. A vote of the General Assembly expelled the United States from this committee and replaced us with Libya, a notorious violator of human rights. This sent a clear message to all human rights violators that no matter what they did the UN was not going to move against those violators in any way.

Some nations blame Russia for the UN's failures, and others blame the United States. Often, the more powerful nations seem to prefer to use their own forces to deal with certain types of conflicts, but this can be easily justified, as the UN seems content to be a debating society.

Another area of weakness is that of financing. Every UN member is expected to pay a share of the expenses, but these are assessed on an ability to pay basis. This formula yields a result in which many small, poorer nations pay practically nothing, while the U.S. pays about twenty-five percent of the total.

Also, the history of the UN is replete with examples where certain nations refused to pay for activities they didn't approve of. Thus, the UN has built up a debt, which has weakened the organization. The U.S. has delayed dues payments contingent on certain reforms.

AND THE LIST GOES ON

The bureaucratic nature of the UN also stymies action. The U.S. has found that the use of their veto power on the Security Council is a threat that sometimes gets results. To avoid lengthy bureaucratic delays and gamesmanship, the U.S. under the G.W. Bush administration threatened to veto all peacekeeping operations for a year to get their own way on relatively minor issues.

Regardless of the UN record, it remains as the premier international organization with a military force. This, along with its ties to the New Age Movement, makes it a logical place for the antichrist to use as a springboard for his plans for world conquest and domination. The EU will actually become a powerful rival to the UN over time, but the UN's role as a truly international organization makes it a logical next step for the antichrist.

The Secretary-General is the administrative head of the UN and has broader powers than any other official. He is nominated by the Security Council and voted on by the General Assembly. The head of a strong European Union, including a viable military force, would be a logical and desirable choice from which to fill this position.

AN ARM OF THE NEW AGE

As previously mentioned, the UN is very New Age-friendly and always has been. There are two organizations that are non-governmental (NGO's) that give assistance, advice, and counsel to the UN. The first is called the Aquarian Age Community, which is code for New Age. They hold their meetings inside the United Nations building in New York. They admit to having many of their people networking in the UN, committed to bring the New World Order into existence. One Christian source states that the "Great being" they expect "will indeed appear" but "will be the antichrist" (contenderministries.org).

The Aquarian Age Community has a great vision for this worldly body of diplomats and delegates. Among their hopes in escorting in the New Age for the UN, they see:

1. The UN exerting a great influence over education. Through new values and principles introduced in schools and through cable and satellite TV, they will teach that which will promote their best interests, including spiritual education.

2. The UN as overseer of all the world's armaments.

3. The United Nations as a place for exerting pressure in the areas of learning a spirit of globalism, an attitude of compromise, and the eventual downfall of nationalism.

4. The UN will be instrumental in bringing about a cashless world.

WHO IS THE "GREAT THINKER"?

The following was taken from the Aquarian Age Community website. "The Aquarian Age Community is dedicated in loving service to humanity, the planet and the 'Great Thinker.' It is inspired by the teachings of master Kool Hoomi, Master Morya, and Master Djwhal Khul as these are set forth in the books of Helena Blavatsky, Alice Bailey and the Agni Yoga Society. These teachings seek to inspire and prepare human consciousness for the great opportunities and possibilities of the 21st century" (Aquarian Age Community 2010, 2).

Some major obstacles for making these goals come true for the New Age Movement are certain divisive religions—Judaism and Christianity. They therefore think that the UN should encourage religious unification, starting with their own members, and find common ground to unite and express all cultures.

On the surface, this would seem unlikely, yet in 2008, Pope Benedict of the Roman Catholic Church was holding meetings with top Muslim ecumenical leaders. No one saw that one coming.

In 2009, the U.S. and Israel refused to attend a UN conference on racism. The document sent out to the various member nations announcing the conference seemed to the U.S. and Israel to be anti-religion in its remarks and generally opposed to the Judeo-Christian worldview. The document strongly implied that exclusive religions were responsible for racism. Needless to say, New Age is very inclusive, accepting an eclectic mix of Eastern and Western thought—except for Judaism and Christianity, that is.

LUCIS TRUST

The second non-government organization that is clearly New Age is Lucis Trust. This is the organization which publishes and disseminates all United Nations material. Lucis Trust was originally established in 1922 as Lucifer Publishing by Alice and Foster Bailey to publish the works of the Theosophical Society, Helena Blavatsky, and Alice Bailey's own writings (Cumbey 1983, 49).

The United Nations Educational, Scientific and Cultural Organization, or UNESCO, is another arm of the UN. "At UNESCO science is seen in terms of service to the whole, demonstrating a working recognition of the oneness of humanity" (World Goodwill Newsletter 1997, 4). The former quote expresses New Age philosophy rather than anything scientific.

According to the Lucis Trust website, "World Goodwill is an accredited, non-governmental organization with the Department of Public Information of the United Nations. World Goodwill is an activity of Lucis Trust, which is on the roster of the United Nations Economic and Security Council." The purpose of the group is: "To co-operate in the world of preparation for Reappearance of the Christ" (*One Earth*, the magazine of the Findhorn Foundation, October/November 1986).

THE MESSAGE IS CLEAR

"Many religions today expect the coming of an Avatar or Savior. The second coming of Christ as the world teacher for the Age of Aquarius, is presented in this book as an eminent event, logical and practical in the continuity of divine revelation throughout the ages. The Christ belongs to all mankind; he can be known and understood as 'the same great identity in all the world religions'" (Bailey 1948, 153).

Their message is clear: There may be one God, but he is called by many names and is worshipped in many ways. This flies in the face of all biblical teaching and is an insult to the only Christ—Jesus. There are many other prominent names associated with this proponent of everything New Age, Lucis Trust, and they have been taking a major role at UN meetings.

One example was Robert Muller, the former Under-Secretary General of the UN. He attended and spoke at hundreds of meetings annually for four decades. His message as the number two man at the UN was consistent, although often couched in New Age terminology; we need a One-World Government and a One-World Religion. In April 1997, in Vancouver British Columbia, Dr Muller stated, "–The truth that was given by Jesus, by Mohammed, by these emissaries from outer space, they were really basic truths. And they were so great that the Cosmos almost incarnated itself–And the Indigenous people, they call it "Great Spirit"...

NGO'S

This will be mighty convenient when it all comes to pass. Don't underestimate these groups; they already have a running start on this agenda, and no one in the United Nations seems to be balking. One-World Government, a global economy, and a universal religion ushering in the Aquarian Age are all attainable goals. As a postscript, this information came from the Aquarian

Age Community website which, by the way, promotes the work of the United Nations.

While the UN has many organizations listed as Non Government Organizations (NGO's), such as AARP and the Baptist World Alliance, everyone knows who these groups are and what they stand for. These organizations are not there to influence the entire direction of the world. When you consider The Aquarian Age and Lucis Trust, you are talking about groups that camouflage their intention using words of peace and love and often Christian terminology.

It takes intense study and research to unravel the New Age agenda. This is a religion that promotes Lucifer or Satan and the antichrist while usually referring to them as "Christ." This is not only misleading, it is a slap in the face of the host nation who predominantly worships the one true God. In promoting and allowing peripheral groups to not only meet at the UN, but to espouse their virtue and creed in subtle phrases, is most deceptive. If their true goal is a One-World Government and One-World Religion (New Age) then it becomes far more than just another NGO housed in the UN.

BUILDING BRIDGES

Add to this the four-decade influence of Robert Muller, who encouraged many NGO's to join the UN to build bridges to as many groups as possible. However, the Under-Secretary was very committed to New Age beliefs and naturally favored NGO's such as The Aquarian Age over more mainstream groups.

There are many other names, groups, and websites that tie the United Nations securely to the New Age and New World

Order. Many believe that there has been a secret conspiracy in place for a very long time; other occult ties often mentioned are Freemasonry, the Illuminati, Greenpeace International, UNICEF, and Amnesty International. The latter three are sponsored by Lucis Trust.

There are many prominent names associated with this dream of a New World Order down through the decades, including presidents of the U.S. No one can be sure of all of their motives; perhaps they really were altruistic. There is no doubt and no secrecy, however, about what many prominent people, like David Rockefeller, thought: "We are on the verge of a global transformation. All we need is the right major crisis, and the nations will accept the New World Order."

THE NEW WORLD ORDER

New World Order is a phrase that has come to signify a conspiracy theory in which a powerful and secretive group is involved in setting up a One-World Government, which they will control. This should not be confused with any proposed form of world government, in which the people of the world have representation. Many mainstream sources tend to view the NWO theorists as conspiracy junkies or just deluded and paranoid. Unfortunately, this is not the case.

The New World Order conspiracy theory holds that many secret NWO organizations have existed over time. Cecil Rhodes (founder of Rhodesia) proposed that the British Empire and the U.S. jointly form a world government to impose world peace. His Rhodes Scholarships were designed to provide the future leaders of the NWO. Bill Clinton was a Rhodes Scholar and a member of the Trilateral Commission (TC).

George W. Bush, whose father and vice president were TC members, initiated the Patriot Act and the Department of Homeland Security after 9/11. These new laws give unprecedented power to our president.

A POPULAR POSITION

Our close friend and ally Great Britain seems to favor an NWO viewpoint. In 2009, Gordon Brown, Prime Minister of the UK, spoke of the "difficult birth pangs of a new global order." And, one more time, in case you are still skeptical of this tapestry of evil that is being woven right before our eyes, please read on.

In a book edited by Dr. Robert Muller, Under-Secretary General of the UN, it is revealed: "Dag Hammarskjold, the rational Nordic economist [and past head of the UN] had ended up as a mystic. He too held at the end of his life that spirituality was the ultimate key to our earthly fate in time and space." But on just what side of spirituality do you want to be? The spirituality Muller was referring to was undoubtedly New Age—the semi-official religion of the UN.

While there are variations on exactly how the NWO will emerge and its primary driving factors, there is an unusual aspect to this conspiracy theory. Not only does it fit Bible prophecy concerning the end times, but some of those purported to be in favor of the NWO agree with the conspiracy theorists. Supporters of the theory claim that certain prominent families are behind this movement—the Rothschilds, the Rockefellers, the Bush family, the Morgans, the Warburgs, the DuPonts, and the Saudi royals.

While most paranoid theories have little factual basis, it is hard to deny something's existence when those who are said to be involved in it agree with the conspiracy theorists. For example, the following statement was made by David Rockefeller, in his book *Memoirs*.

> Some even believe we (the Rockefeller family) are part of a secret cabal working against the best interests of the United States, characterizing my family and me as "internationalists" and of conspiring with others around the world to build a more integrated global political and economic structure—one world, if you will. If that's the charge, I stand guilty, and I am proud of it.
>
> Rockefeller 2002, 405

Notice that he not only is admitting to doing this, but he is also saying that he is not working in the best interests of the U.S. At some point, conspiracy theories start to look like conspiracy facts. What did David Rockefeller actually do to support this line of thinking?

THE TRILATERAL COMMISSION NATIONALLY

In 1973, Rockefeller established the Trilateral Commission as a high-level private global think tank with about 325 distinguished business and political leaders from the U.S., Europe and Japan. This included top people from politics, academia, and other disciplines. Some of the objectives of this new organization were "remaking world trade," "managing the world economy," and "improving the chances of a smooth and peaceful evolution of the global system."

It sounds like Rockefeller was certainly out to change our global society from one of nation states to some kind of New World Order. Specific meeting topics of the TC and detailed agenda are kept secret. However, it seems logical, based upon the makeup of the organization and statements of its members, that they see themselves as creating a one-world political system run by the elite.

You might be interested in knowing just a few names of people who were members of the Trilateral Commission: Jimmy Carter, George H.W. Bush, Dick Cheney, Bill Clinton, John Glenn, Alan Greenspan, Paul Volcker, Alexander Haig, Henry Kissinger, Walter Mondale, and Casper Weinberger. Notice that members of this group seem to do very well in U.S. politics.

The list also includes many leaders of this nation over the past few decades. It seems that members of the Trilateral Commission have had ready access to the corridors of power in Washington DC. In fact, the Carter administration was criticized in the mainstream media for appointing so many Commission members to important foreign policy posts. Reagan was not a member, but the senior Bush was. Bill Clinton was a member, as was Dick Cheney.

Thus, from 1980 up until the Obama administration, there has always been a president or a vice president of the U.S. who served at one time as a Commission member. A few other high-ranking names you might recognize include Lloyd Benston, Warren Christopher, Henry Cisneros, Lawrence Eagleburger, Diane Feinstein, Brent Scowcroft, William Scranton, Donna Shalala, and Robert Taft, Jr. It appears that membership in this private group, which wants our nation states to evolve into a global society, is a great step forward for a career as a U.S. politician.

A POWERFUL GROUP

The Obama administration tapped Trilateral Commission member Paul Volcker to chair his economic advisory panel. Obama sought advice from this group on how to stabilize financial markets. More importantly, Obama picked Zbigniew Brzezinski as his top foreign policy advisor. He was a protégé of Henry Kissinger and David Rockefeller and is responsible for the actual establishment of the Trilateral Commission. He was also a high-ranking official in the Carter administration—one of twenty-six members or former members of the TC in the Carter White House.

As for Obama, he announced during his summer 2008 visit to Germany, "Tonight, I speak to you not as a candidate for President but as a citizen—a proud citizen of the United States and a fellow citizen of the world." That sounds very New World Order-friendly. News media types also noted that the American flag on the tail of Obama's aircraft had been replaced by his campaign logo and that he spoke in front of the victory column, which represents Germany's conquests of the past.

So the impact of the Commission on our national government continues. From an unbiased look at the facts, it seems that the TC has been far too powerful an influence on our nation's politics, especially in the foreign policy area. Once again, it is wise to ask the question so many Americans are wondering about: Why have we been involved in two land wars in Asia?

THE TC INTERNATIONALLY

The TC appears to view the banking system and the UN as possible unifying factors. However, politicians are a problem in that they are motivated by the quest for power rather than other objectives such as a smoothly functioning world government. "The politicians have looked to the UN for a different reason. Politicians seek power. Control over their own government is all too often only a beginning to their ambition. History is littered with corpses who mutely testify to the imperial ambitions and arrogance of politicians" (Berkman 1993, 7).

The UN also has this objective in mind but can see this as a somewhat more democratic institution making up kind of a United States of the World. Most sovereign powers will be transferred to the UN. They also see religion as a possible unifying factor for this was the vision of Under-Secretary Robert Muller, the number two man in the UN for four decades.

When we connect the dots, certain conclusions seem inescapable. The Trilateral Commission, the UN, the EU, and New Age more than fit together; they actually overlap in many important aspects. They all support the concept of a One-World Government and a reduction of the sovereign powers of today's nation states. Also various people seem to move effortlessly between and among these groups. Why is it that the UN would choose the New Age religion, at best a group of pagans, as the one they favor and promote? Could the answer be that both the UN and New Age have the same ultimate goal—that everyone on the planet is part of their two groups?

The New Age religion is important in that it appears to embrace all religions (except Judaism and Christianity) and can be a unifying factor in creating a New World Order. While they see New Agers running the One-World Government through religion, they also recognize the need for political leadership and thus have developed a close relationship with the UN. These groups together have enough in common and have laid enough groundwork to bridge the relatively minor gaps between them and act in concert to form a One-World Government, which will become the final vehicle to ultimate power for the antichrist.

CONSOLIDATION THE GOAL

The various groups may have somewhat different versions of how they see the New World Order. However, compromise, a little give and take, in some areas to achieve the greater end is likely. The EU will adjust to being a regional sector of the UN. The Trilateral Commission will see the logic of utilizing the only viable world entity, the UN, complete with New Age as part of the package. New Age will continue to claim they embrace Buddha, Allah, Krishna, et al., as the Christ, thus proving they are all-inclusive. Those who favor the NWO will literally sell their souls and accept these changes as the nation states have slowly reduced their sovereign powers in Europe.

The following quote made back in 1964 seems to sum up the connection and direction that all four of these organizations are heading. The statement was made by Senator Barry Goldwater:

> The Trilateral Commission is intended to be the vehicle for multinational consolidation of the commercial and banking interests by seizing control of the political government of the United States. The Trilateral Commission represents a skillful, coordinated effort to seize control and consolidate

the four centers of power–Political, Monetary, Intellectual, and Ecclesiastical.

(Goldwater 1964, 280)

According to this statement, the plan all hinges on gaining or "seizing control" in the U.S., which will lead directly to "multinational consolidation."

IT'S ALL COMING TOGETHER

So now the background needed to understand the present and, therefore, building the bridge that will go from the past to the future has been covered. It is important that we all realize the common thread that runs between the EU, the Trilateral Commission, and the United Nations is the New Age philosophy.

The eight Millennium Goals, which all 192 Member States of the UN have agreed upon, include praiseworthy aims such as eradicating poverty, hunger, and disease. However, it is the last two that show the true direction this agency would like to take. They are to ensure environmental sustainability and to develop a global partnership for development. While these, too, seem laudable, the only way they can be accomplished is through some type of worldwide effort, which in turn requires a powerful worldwide authority to carry this out. In short, the current UN run by a dictator.

Please bear in mind that the UN has a court system already in place. The International Court of Justice, located in The Hague, Netherlands, is the main court and is set up to adjudicate disputes among states. This court has heard cases related to war crimes, ethnic cleansing, and the like. However, there appears to be no reason why the activities of the court could not be expanded under a strong leader at the UN. Already, a new court—the International Criminal Court—has authority to try individuals charged with war crimes and genocide.

Hitler always boasted he did everything legally. You can bet that the antichrist will want to do the same. So the stage has been set, prophecy has been fulfilled, and technology and New Age ideologies are firmly in place to rush us into the New World Order. It's all coming together as a globalized world looks to the economic advantages of a connected world and overlooks the downside.

The antichrist, being a charismatic speaker and a polished political pro as the leader of the EU, embracing all the New Age philosophies and spewing out their rhetoric, will have no trouble convincing the UN he should run it and that he can solve its many problems. It is more than likely that he will be a member of the power elite and will be courted by the TC until he accepts their invitation, thus completing the circle. His message as a person with a plan for world peace will be well received. His record in the EU will be most impressive. Once in power, he will rule the entire world as a dictator.

BE ALERT AND WISE

There is something surreal about all of this. It's as if people are in the process of wrapping the earth and its inhabitants in some glittery paper. This gift looks wonderful as it is paraded before the citizenry of the world. However, as it is presented, it will be skillfully switched. Then, the silver tongue of the antichrist will say of its contents—if indeed there are any, "Look how beautiful this is, and it all belongs to you!" In actuality, it is we who are giving him the present. We are unceremoniously handing over the world, joined together by New Age glue that has a smooth, sweet, Pollyanna veneer to it.

In the eighties, there was a very popular TV show called *The A Team*. The team accomplished what seemed to be impossible tasks, and when they were victorious, their leader would say, "I love it when a plan comes together!" Well, you're watching one come together right before your eyes—a diabolical one with more twists and turns than a roller coaster, but it's finally heading home, and every new step illuminates this plan a little more. It's been said that there are none so blind as those who will not see. It's time we opened our eyes and really saw what's going on all around us!

Everyone needs to be careful, as many will fall into step behind those sincere people who have been touting a New World Order for decades, lest well-meaning people come one step closer to helping the beast reach his goal of world domination. No one knows for sure if anything can stop the inevitable; however, in being wise, in being aware, people can protect themselves and their loved ones. If people ignorantly dismiss this group as just another fanatical organization, they make the same mistake that was made in Nazi Germany. Do not underestimate the enemy; all the forces of hell are behind him.

ALL THE PLAYERS

The EU, the UN, the Trilateral Commission, and the New Age philosophy and religion are all vehicles that stand ready to assist the antichrist in attaining his position as world dictator. As natural and spiritual powers come together, the end of days will be upon us quicker than we think. The Bible uses the phrase as "a thief in the night."

The facts show that this NWO seems less like a conspiracy and more like a well-coordinated movement to weaken nation-state sovereignty so that One-World Government can emerge. Make no mistake about it, people are sheep and easily led by a charismatic leader saying all the things we would like to hear. Will there be much objection to trading away a little more sovereignty for the promise of lasting world peace? The NWO groups are in place and set up to make sure our objections are muted and suppressed. Remember that a whole nation listened to and followed the racial rantings of a madman named Adolf Hitler.

There is yet one last player, the man who fits neatly into the power elite mindset·and the NWO and his philosophy of neo-Nazism. The one who set the almost perfect pattern for evil, Adolf Hitler has been *the* man that has been mentioned numerous times in this book as someone who many thought, at the time, was the antichrist. And he is certainly history's prime example of the type of arrogant, conscienceless, egomaniacal figure we see pictured in Revelation as the antichrist. But who exactly was this madman and how can we glean a picture of the future through him?

CHAPTER FOUR:

HITLER—AN AMBITIOUS DESPOT

TO LOOK AT THE PAST
OF DIABOLICAL SIN

IS TO LOOK AT THE FUTURE.
WE'LL BE WHERE WE'VE BEEN.

The year was 1889, and it was uneventful as far as history was concerned. Some of the highlights include the patenting of the coin pay telephone by William Gray, King Menelik of Shoa being made King of Ethiopia, and Kipling returning to England and being proclaimed literary heir to Dickens. Many non-events seemed to mark the year 1889.

There was, however, one important thing that took place in April. It happened in a quaint town in Austria, just across the river from Germany: Adolf Hitler was born. There was a twenty-four-year age difference between his father and his mother, who were second cousins. Hitler's mother's name was Klara, and his father was Alois. His paternal grandmother was Anna Schicklgruber, who was not married when she gave birth to Alois. This is why Adolf was teased and taunted as Adolf Schicklgruber. His grandmother eventually married a miller named Hiedler, who took responsibility for Alois. However, Alois spelled his new last name H-i-t-l-e-r (Geocities.com 2003, 1)

HITLER THE BOY

When Adolf was six years old, he entered the first grade, and his father retired on a pension from the Austrian civil service. Unfortunately, this meant a double dose of supervision from his strict father. He was an authoritarian who was used to giving orders and expected his household to be regimented. Adolf, his brother, his sister, his parents, his half-brother, and his half-sister lived in a small farmhouse. His father found adjusting to retirement difficult and often took out his discontent on his oldest son, Alois. At age fourteen, Alois, tired of being mistreated, ran away from home. This left young Adolf next in line to bear his father's abuse.

Adolf attended school in an old Catholic Benedictine monastery, and he idolized the priests. At one time, he even considered becoming a priest. As a child, he was an avid reader and was especially taken with the writings of a German author named Karl May. May wrote of a cowboy hero named Old Shatterhand, who was brave and won all the battles over the Indians. This had a profound effect on Adolf. He read and reread all of the seventy novels in the series well into adulthood.

Real confrontations between Adolf and his father began to occur when it came time to choose a secondary school. His father wanted him to go to a technical high school while Adolf, who had aspirations of becoming an artist, wanted to go to classical school. His father prevailed and sent the twelve-year-old off to the big city to school. Adolf did not fit in and did so poorly his first year that they kept him back.

The battles between Adolf and Alois persisted and grew more and more bitter. In his second year, Adolf became a ringleader, as he had been in grade school, since he was a full year older than his classmates. Though he was Austrian, they lived very close to the German border, and he aligned himself—in defiance of his father—with the Germans. Adolf and his friends went so far as to use the German greeting, "Heil," and sang the German national anthem instead of the Austrian one. Perhaps part of this rebellion can be traced back to his father's staunch support of the Austrian monarchy. Whatever the reason, Adolf soon had another obsession: German nationalism.

HITLER THE TEEN

Young Hitler was just thirteen when his father died from a lung hemorrhage. It was very sudden, and it left the teen as the male head of the household. With his father gone, so was the discipline and regimentation of Adolf's life. He got poor grades and behaved badly. He played pranks and practical jokes aimed at his teachers, and he left school before he was thrown out. He enrolled in another school but didn't do much better there; by age sixteen, he had dropped out for good.

Hitler was finally free to pursue his art career. He took the entrance exam at the Academy of Fine arts in Vienna, but he failed. His mother became gravely ill and suffered greatly with cancer over the next year. When she finally died, Hitler was devastated.

Now officially an orphan, eighteen-year-old Adolf moved to Vienna with the hope of being accepted to the art academy. There, his habits and personality began to reveal more of his quirks. He was lazy and refused to even look for a job. He would sleep until noon and then go for a walk to take in the sights.

He would stay up to all hours having debates and discussions on his ideas on almost any subject. He considered himself above any regular job. He dressed like an artist, and at night, he dressed up and often attended the opera. He was nineteen when he tried for the second time to gain admittance to the art academy. This time, his test drawings were judged so poorly that they didn't even permit him to take the entrance exam. It was a bitter disappointment for Hitler.

HITLER THE YOUNG MAN

As his savings dwindled, he moved from place to place, each room a little worse than the one before. Despite his desperate state, he never tried to get employment. Eventually, he pawned everything he owned and slept on park benches in his tattered clothes. He became a beggar—dirty and unshaven. In freezing December 1909, he moved into a homeless shelter and ate at a nearby soup kitchen.

For the next few years, Hitler lived in a home for the poor. He sometimes earned a little money by doing menial tasks and selling his pictures on the street. Eventually, a Jewish shop owner and avid occultist, Josef Neumann, displayed some of Hitler's paintings in his store.

The years of his unhappy childhood, especially his relationship with his father and an over-attachment to his indulgent mother, were beginning to show in the adult Adolf. He experienced hysterical outbursts and bouts of depression as well as extreme highs that eventually sunk back into depression.

Hitler loved to read and often spent his afternoons in a library. He had a habit of reading the philosophies of various complex authors such as Nietzsche, Fichte, or Houston Chamberlain and taking bits and pieces of each. To this he added a new interest in the occult, and he became obsessed with anti-Semite literature, even though he kept some Jewish friends who helped sell his art. He learned to hate the multicultural Austrian Empire and also hated the government for which his father worked. Rather than serve in the army, Hitler left Vienna. From this conglomeration of ideas, Hitler formed his own anti-Semitic, racist, nationalist, power hungry philosophy.

HITLER THE SOLDIER

Hitler moved to Munich, Germany. He continued to paint local scenes and sell his paintings to local shops. On August 1, 1914, Germany proclaimed war. Two days later, Hitler enlisted in a Bavarian regiment of the German Army. Hitler finally found a place to belong. His life had purpose and meaning, and it was called World War I.

Hitler was a brave soldier who often put himself in harm's way, yet somehow he always managed to dodge serious injury. After one engagement, 2,500 of the 3,000 men in Hitler's regiment were killed, wounded, or missing, but Hitler didn't have a scratch. He constantly walked away from life-threatening situations when all around him dropped. His great luck continued through the entire war, even though he had the dangerous job of bicycle courier and was often at the front lines, delivering messages.

Hitler was a most unconventional soldier. He had a sloppy manner and was not at all military in his bearing. He was eager, however, and always volunteered for dangerous assignments. But because of his appearance and strange personality, Hitler never rose beyond the rank of corporal, though he was awarded the Iron Cross by a Jewish officer. He had a total of five medals when the war ended.

When the war was over and Germany had lost, Hitler blamed the loss on the politicians—primarily the Jews and Marxists. Hitler eventually became an informant and under-cover agent in the German Army. He named soldiers in his barracks who supposedly supported the Marxist uprising, which began to take place in Munich. He helped weed out Marxist influences within the ranks.

In 1919, Hitler was given the job of lecturing returning German prisoners of war on the dangers of communism and pacifism. He also spoke against democracy and disobedience, but his most fiery speeches were saved for the Jews. He would rant against the Jews and their part in the defeat of Germany. During these assignments, Hitler realized he had a real talent for public speaking.

HITLER THE SPEECH-MAKER

Hitler was next assigned to investigate the German Workers' Party. Hitler recognized the great opportunity inherent in this small, disorganized group. He liked the idea that they wanted to become more than a political party—they wanted to become a movement. Hitler joined the German Workers' Party and thus began his political career.

Hitler eventually helped their numbers grow as he became a strong speaker for the party. His anti-Semitic, anti-communist ravings made him the main attraction at the meetings, which were held in the local beer halls. His orations fascinated many maladjusted soldiers looking for excitement, and they joined the party in record numbers. The meetings grew, thanks to some shrewd planning and advertising by Herr Hitler, and soon the Workers' Party was attracting thousands.

Hitler changed the name of the party to the National Socialist German Workers' Party (Nationalsozialistische Deutsche Arbeit-erpartei or NSDAP), which was shortened to Nazi (The History Place 1996, 1) and designed a flag as a symbol. He took the swastika, a decoration he had seen on the monastery walls at his school, and put it in a white circle with a red background. The swastika had also been seen as an emblem for other anti-Semitic parties, as well as for certain occult philosophies. Combined with the white and red, it was a powerful symbol that helped the new movement gain prestige and popularity.

By the beginning of 1921, the party had three thousand members. It was in July 1921 that Hitler was first officially called the *führer* of the Nazi Party. Hitler became well known for his tirades and his anti-Semitic speeches, and the party grew.

HITLER THE REVOLUTIONARY

Between 1921 and 1923, an economic crisis occurred in Germany. In November 1923, the German mark fell to 4,000,000,000,000 to the dollar, when it was once four marks to the dollar. Germans lost everything. Their money was worthless, and so were their salaries. Exorbitant prices made it impossible to buy food. People went hungry, and riots broke out. It all began when France and England presented a bill to Germany for damages caused by the war. The bill was for thirty-three billion dollars for reparations. The German government simply printed the money, which started a downward spiral of events that led to hyper-inflation, hunger, resentment, and chaos.

The Nazis felt this was the time to strike. Hitler had a plan to kidnap leaders of the Bavarian government and force them to accept him as their leader. Then, they would win over the German Army, lead a national revolt, and bring down the entire German government. The plan was scheduled to go into effect on November 8, 1923. While it appeared that the kidnaping of the Bavarian leaders in a beer hall where they were all gathered seemed like a good plan, it wasn't long before it all fell apart, and the revolution fizzled. This thwarted takeover became known as the Beer Hall Putsch, or revolution.

Hitler was put on trial for high treason, but unfortunately it was not the end of his political career, as many had predicted. There was great press coverage, and Hitler became a nationally known figure. He spoke long and often at his trial, and this man who could have gotten life imprisonment wound up winning over the judge and everyone else. His prison stay was more like a country club event. He had a large, private cell with a great view, and he was allowed to receive visitors. Hitler ended up serving nine months, during which time he dictated his book, *Mein Kampf*—"my struggle"—to his prison private secretary, Rudolf Hess.

Hitler was released from prison just before Christmas in 1924. He had a lot of time while he was incarcerated to meditate on the mistakes he made that led to jail. He realized that overthrowing the government was not the way to go. Then, he decided he would reorganize the party itself so that it would become a government in waiting, ready to be put into place when the opportunity presented itself.

HITLER AT REST

Things got better for Germany, and as the economy improved, the German people became more satisfied with their democratic government. This meant that Hitler and the Nazi Party had to bide their time. Hitler found a beautiful retreat in the mountains in Bavaria. He spent the years 1926 through 1929 there, with peaceful musings and inspiring views, knowing his time would come. It was there that he finished dictating the second volume of *Mein Kampf* to Rudolf Hess. Hitler was thirty-nine when he invited his stepsister to come live with him. She arrived with her two daughters, Friedl and Geli.

Hitler's niece Geli, a lovely twenty-year-old, quickly won her uncle's heart. He fell madly in love with her and took her with him everywhere he went. At first, the girl was flattered by the overwhelming attention and by the power her uncle wielded; however, she soon tired of the constant and watchful eye of Hitler and his bodyguards. She felt stifled and wanted to leave. Hitler adamantly refused her and practically locked her up whenever he left town and couldn't take her with him. His overbearing manner and possessive love finally drove Geli to suicide. This threw Hitler into a state of grief.

During this time, Hitler found a real jewel in one Joseph Goebbels. He was brilliant and had a PhD in literature. He was a most talented man who got things done in the fields of speech-making and propaganda. He quickly rose through the hierarchy of the Nazi Party. Goebbels was very efficient in many areas, including generating great publicity to get his party recognition.

HITLER THE CANDIDATE

The wake-up call for Hitler came in October of 1929. Who could have predicted that an event that occurred halfway around the world would create an opening for the now greatly expanded Nazi Party? Across the ocean in New York City, the stock market crashed. Its effects were devastating in America and eventually worldwide.

Unemployment soared, and hunger and poverty grew. People panicked, and fear was king. Governments were on the brink of disaster and could seemingly do little about this international economic collapse. It was the beginning of the Great Depression, and Hitler saw that his time was at hand. In 1931 and 1932, there was much behind-the-scenes jockeying for position where German politics were concerned. There were deals made and broken, all in an effort to get Hitler into the headship of Germany. The Nazi Party grew strong and powerful.

The *Sturmabteilung,* also known as the SA—or Hitler's storm troopers—then numbered almost half a million. They were organized and ready for a revolution. They roamed the streets of Germany in their impressive uniforms—they were sometimes called the "brownshirts"—wreaking more havoc as fights and chaos broke out all over. The Nazis gained control of the Reichstag, or German Parliament.

Changes in the German government came often—so often that the people were tired of elections. The state of the economy and the instability and inability of the government to do anything significant played right into Hitler's hands. In March 1932, he decided to run for President of Germany. Although he lost, it was a moral victory for Hitler; he garnered thirty percent of the vote and made a runoff election imminent. In the runoff, his opponent Hindenburg won by an absolute majority, but this time Hitler had well over thirteen million votes, or thirty-seven percent. His margin was creeping up, and Hitler was pleased with his progress. He knew that it was just a matter of time.

HITLER THE POLITICIAN

Meanwhile, in Hitler's personal life, his young girlfriend Eva Braun attempted suicide. It brought back a flood of memories about his niece's death, and Hitler rushed to her side. She loved him madly, but she could not get the attention from Hitler that she craved. Even though time away from politics slowed down the Nazi campaign, he stayed by her side until she recovered.

By now, the German republic was unstable, and fear and disorder gripped the nation. A scheming, ambitious army officer hatched a plan with Hitler to get the German Chancellor to resign. They were successful, and that resignation put Hitler's army friend in control. But he chose someone other than Hitler as his Chancellor, someone he, Hitler's friend, could control. As the treachery mounted, violence and murder escalated in the streets.

As the July elections approached, the Nazis campaigned at a frenetic pace. Hitler spoke to crowds of millions. He promised them everything and anything. He even told them that he would make sure every unmarried girl found a husband. His strategy worked, and the Nazi Party became the largest and mightiest in Germany.

The plotting and scheming continued behind the scenes, and with the Nazis in control of the Reichstag, the German government was not workable. The Chancellor resigned, and Hitler demanded his position. His demand was denied by von Hindenburg for the second time, and instead, Hitler's treacherous conspirator was made Chancellor. After more plotting and wrangling, President Hindenburg, in his dotage, was finally persuaded to appoint Adolf Hitler Chancellor of Germany.

HITLER THE CHANCELLOR

Hitler was to preside over a cabinet that had ten positions and only two other Nazis. This was, of course, part of the plan by the opposition to keep Hitler in line. Each group that backed Hitler had their own agenda. The one thing they all had in common was that they all underestimated him.

Not everyone was taken in by Hitler's speech-making and the pomp and circumstance that accompanied him. Former General Erich Ludendorff, a one-time supporter of Hitler, sent the following telegram to President Hindenburg:

> By appointing Hitler Chancellor of the Reich, you have handed over our sacred Fatherland to one of the greatest demagogues of all time. I prophecy to you this evil man will plunge our *reich* into the abyss and will inflict immeasurable woe on our nation. Future generations will curse you in your grave for this action.

Nothing could stop Hitler now. Once he was firmly in place, he had no intention of following the rules of democracy. The SA joined forces with a deranged Dutch Communist Marinus van der

Lubbe and burned down the Reichstag. This event helped to trump up charges against the Communists. It wasn't long before there was a roundup of people by the truckload. Thousands of Communists, Social Democrats, and liberals were taken into "protective custody"—to SA camps—where they were severely abused.

On March 5, 1933, elections took place, and the Nazis received forty-four percent of the total vote. Despite all the plotting and scheming, and regardless of all the treachery, Hitler was still denied a majority. However, that didn't stop him and his ruthless thugs from throwing out legitimate officeholders and replacing them with Nazis. Thousands of political enemies were rounded up, arrested, and held in old army barracks and abandoned factories. This was the start of the Nazi concentration camps.

HITLER THE DICTATOR

There was one final action that Hitler craved. He desperately wanted to have his Enabling Act passed by the Reichstag. If it passed, it would establish the legal dictatorship of Adolf Hitler. The SA stood by, intimidating anyone who would not vote for the act. Hitler gave a stirring speech in which he pledged not to abuse these new powers and promised to promote peace and end unemployment. The vote was taken; the measure passed 441 to 84. The Nazis immediately rose to their feet and began to applaud, stomp their feet, and shout. They had brought down democracy—legally.

Hindenburg's death in 1934 put together the offices of President and Chancellor and cemented Hitler's dictatorship. The death knell of the democratic state was still reverberating as Hitler began to come to grips with his hatred for the Jews. He convinced himself and millions of other Germans that the Jews were primarily responsible for Germany's many problems in the years during and following World War I. He told gross lies, and the German people believed him. A progressive program was put into effect that would at first strip the Jews of all their rights and, at last, annihilate the entire race. Ironically, the oath that Hitler swore for his post as Chancellor was: "I will employ my strength for the welfare of the German people, protect the Constitution and laws…and conduct my affairs–with justice for everyone" (Geocities.com 2003, 1).

THE ORDEAL OF THE JEWS

It is here that we must take a breather and realize how well this fits into Bible prophecy. The Jews, after all, were God's chosen people. It was foretold that they were the ones who were to spend most of their time on Earth wandering and being persecuted wherever they went (Ezekiel 36:19, 24).

History certainly bears witness to the veracity and extent of this 2,600-year-old prophecy. From the Babylonian and Roman Empire and the Crusades to the Spanish Inquisition and the Holocaust, Jews have been displaced, enslaved, tortured, and murdered. Only in recent history have they finally been restored to their homeland, coming from the four corners of the earth to reclaim their inheritance. No prophecy has been more played out on the stage of life than this.

It was the autumn of 1933 when Jews began to systematically lose all rights in Germany. As their civil rights disappeared, it became more and more evident that their human rights were next. Jobs were denied to Jews, and curfews imposed.

During that same time, a massive smear campaign was launched in the media by Propaganda Minister Joseph Goebbels. He made sure that Jews were portrayed as enemies of the German people. State-sanctioned anti-Semitic slurs appeared in every German forum; it became the norm throughout Germany. Synagogues were destroyed on the flimsiest of excuses, and property was confiscated.

THE HORROR BEGINS

If there was one night that marked the beginning of the Holocaust, it was November 9, 1938. It is called *Kristallnacht*—the Night of Broken Glass. It was precipitated by Herschel Grynszpan, the seventeen-year-old son of a Polish Jew. In retaliation for the harsh treatment of his parents, he shot and killed a German embassy official. The Nazis used the death of Von Rath as an excuse to lead the first state-run massacre against Jews. Ninety Jews were killed, five hundred synagogues were burned, and almost all Jewish businesses were damaged. It was also the first mass arrest for Jews; over twenty-five thousand men were taken to concentration camps. To put an exclamation point on the event, the Nazis fined the Jews one billion marks for the damages the Nazis caused.

There was nothing that Hitler would not blame on the Jews. He was about to instigate a new world war, and he intended to blame it on the Jews. He said in a speech in Berlin:

> Today I will once more be a prophet: if the international Jewish financiers in and outside Europe should succeed in plunging the nations once more into a world war, then the result will not be the Bolshevizing of the earth, and thus a victory of Jewry, but the annihilation of the Jewish race in Europe!

It was 1938 when Hitler, with his beefed-up army, absorbed Austria into Germany. That same year, he began a takeover of Czechoslovakia that ended in March of 1939. In September of 1939, German troops stormed into Poland. After Poland's quick defeat, the Germans rounded up their three million Jews and forced them into ghettos in Warsaw, Krakow, and Lodz. In 1940, the Germans built a concentration camp in Auschwitz that housed Polish Jews to provide slave labor for German factories.

HITLER AT WAR

As a direct result of Hitler invading Poland, France and England declared war on Germany in September of 1939. This was the onset of World War II. Hitler's armies easily conquered Denmark, Norway, Belgium, Luxembourg, and the Netherlands. It was about this time that Italy, Germany's Axis ally under the dictatorship of Mussolini, declared war on France and England. By June 1940, France had surrendered, and Britain stood alone.

Hitler expected England to surrender, but they kept fighting. German armies then invaded Russia in June of 1941. Three million Germans encountered continued resistance, and that, combined with the bitterly cold weather, stopped the Germans outside of Moscow.

In December of 1941, the United States was drawn into the war when the Japanese—one of the members of the Axis powers—bombed Pearl Harbor, Hawaii. The U.S., in response, poured huge amounts of supplies into Britain and Russia. This was the beginning of the end for Hitler and the Third Reich. It wasn't long until the Allies drove the Japanese from Asia, and the Russians were pushing the German Army back toward Germany. In

June 1944, a huge Allied force invaded Europe. Hitler panicked and ordered death for any soldier who retreated.

HITLER DOES THE WORLD A FAVOR

Meanwhile, Hitler and his henchmen continued exterminating Jews at a frenzied pace. Railroad cars that were badly needed by the German Army were used instead to transport Jews to Auschwitz. A mass deportation of Jews began in May of 1944 and continued until July. Almost half a million Hungarian Jews were deported to Auschwitz during this time, and they recorded the highest number of killings and cremations—over nine thousand in one day. Numerous large pits were dug to burn the bodies, since the number of dead was greater than the capacity of the crematories.

The Bible once again proved its prophetic ability. Jeremiah 16:4a states: "They shall die gruesome deaths; they shall not be lamented nor shall they be buried, but they shall be like refuse on the face of the earth". Written about 2,600 years ago, this prophecy is a most accurate depiction of the Holocaust. At the time, its graphic description must have seemed unfathomable to the author.

As the Allies pushed into Germany in the spring of 1945, they liberated those camps that were left. Only then did the full horror of their diabolical secrets become apparent as survivors gave accounts of the inhumane treatment, torture, and death of the six million Jews and other "undesirables."

On April 30, 1945, Adolf Hitler did the world a favor and committed suicide along with his new wife, Eva Braun. Hitler's aides burned their bodies. Seven days later, Germany surrendered. The victorious Allies then began the horrible task of sorting through the carnage to determine responsibility. The Nuremberg trials began seven months later. There were twenty-two high-ranking Nazis charged with crimes against humanity.

MY REVERIE

We have heard all the terrible adjectives before—hate-mongers, atrocities, etc.—but to those of us who didn't live through World War II, they are, after all, just words. Once we turn off the TV after watching something like *Schindler's List*, the sadness envelopes us once more. We shake our heads in disbelief and wonder, half aloud, how any human being could even imagine perpetrating such horror on fellow humans. Of course, in the case of Nazi Germany, the general public pleaded ignorance, but it still took thousands to make such a plan happen.

These were the thoughts that went through my mind as I strolled the meticulous streets of Munich barely thirty years after the horror that was named World War II. If I hadn't taken the time to read every article and watch every broadcast—every detail of this crazy time—perhaps I could have enjoyed my vacation more.

The ambiance was pleasant enough, and the people were more than friendly. The architecture in Munich was generally Gothic, and buildings that had been destroyed were reconstructed in their same style. Outside of the city, the surrounding countryside was beautiful and mountainous, and the roads were dotted with hikers strolling to their favorite wooded picnic spot.

The streets in Munich were narrow and curvy and often one-way. Downtown was overrun with small specialty shops with all the German-made products peering out from behind their glass. Cuckoo clocks were a big seller and could be seen in a variety of sizes and shapes. Shopkeepers greeted me, often with brooms in their hands, since they are compulsively tidy in Munich. These shops were located in large plazas that also served beer—another famous German export.

HITLER'S HAUNTS

The beer halls too were scrubbed down daily, and the restrooms were spotless. The Bavarian beer halls were much bigger and much noisier than I expected, and they had many long, narrow tables, where patrons could get to know their neighbors. The servers were all women in centuries-old costumes with apron fronts, and the beer was served in large liter steins. Singing and raucous talk and laughter filled the rooms and echoed off the tiled floors and walls. The beer halls—nothing evoked a stronger reminder of how it all began over a half century ago than visiting these large establishments with their high ceilings, many windows, and easy-to-clean tile on the walls.

As I sat in one such beer hall in the 1970s, I let my imagination wander. It was the late twenties in my mind, and the subject was politics and remained so through the years. A little-known, relatively young man named Hitler captivated the crowd of almost a thousand people with his strong words and great speech-making. It was a strange, yet fitting beginning for an ambitious person who would rule the world—at least in his mind.

I could see him shouting, then pausing for effect, and hypnotizing the crowd so that they swayed to the meter of his speech. His gift for speaking was uncanny, and he held a strange, seductive spell over his audience. It was hard to believe that what began somewhat innocently in a beer hall, much like the one I sat in on that day, ended with thousands of men—German men—who were more than happy to carry out demonic orders and murder six million people.

But it was more than murder, if that's possible; they were stripped of all their rights as human beings and degraded to the point that certain death was often a welcome relief. Their corpses were flung about in a manner that one uses to throw out the trash.

My reverie abruptly ended—and I was grateful for that—by a waitress gleefully asking me if I wanted another beer in her oft-practiced but broken English. I couldn't help but wonder, though, what could possibly be the rationale for such abhorrent actions? How does one think of such darkness, let alone carry it out?

IT TOOK PLANNING

This systematic program for purifying the German race was implemented with precision in the first three decades of the twentieth century. By the thirties, all was in place. There were many forces at work. Back as far as the eighteenth century, economists, historians, scientists, and doctors discussed things like too many people, too little food, keeping races pure, and prisoners and mental patients and those suffering from incurable conditions being a drain on society. These mind-sets produced a brotherhood that embraced and supported Herr Hitler and his forward-thinking concepts, which just happened to coincide with their own. It didn't hurt that his new religion, the occult, embraced many New Age philosophies and welcomed these issues and policies.

Joseph Carr in his book *The Twisted Cross* states, "One cannot argue against the claim that the Nazi world view and major elements of the New Age Movement are identical. They should be, after all, for they both grew out of the same occult root: theosophy. Their respective cosmology and philosophies are identical."

In June of 1933, at a scientific gathering dealing with eugenics (racial hygiene), Wilhelm Frick, Minister of the Interior, reported that one in five Germans was unsound. He went on to say that these people should be prevented from reproducing, since their offspring would be undesirable. It was only one month later—only four months after the Nazis were brought to power—that the Sterilization Law was passed. This law took effect on January 5, 1934. The law was clear and precise and a very real step toward Hitler's attainment of his "pure and superior" Germanic race. The Sterilization Law covered most hereditary diseases and even included those suffering from severe alcoholism.

MAKING IT ALL LEGAL

An entire legal system was set up called *Erbgesundheitgerichte,* or Hereditary Health Court. This court could rule that sterilization should be carried out, even if against a person's will, and that applying force was permissible. As the new law and the court flourished under Nazi rule, they became more brazen. In November of 1934, they decided that "habitual offenders against public morals" were to be castrated; this included "racial pollution." Unfortunately, this was only the beginning of Hitler's ambitious plan.

Before 1933, any anti-Semitic acts by the Nazis would have been illegal under the German Constitution. Once the Nazis were in power, anti-Jewish legislation began to flood the new government. It began with the forced retirement of non-Aryan government employees. It reached its pinnacle with the Nuremberg Laws in September of 1935. These two laws were aimed at rooting out all non-Aryan elements.

Hitler had a lot of help instituting these new laws. The basic ideas of sterilization and euthanasia came from the psychiatric community. In fact, they were supported worldwide by many groups with an interest in the progressive development of mental hygiene. While many other countries had such support groups, including the United States, Germany was the only nation who had the political climate to carry out these fringe ideas to unbelievable heights.

The "mercy killings" soon escalated. It was a great opportunity to play God and get rid of anybody who wasn't worthy of life. According to some experts, at least fifty percent of those murdered would have recovered and led useful lives had they been allowed to live. Much planning and deceit went into keeping these things quiet from the German public. To Hitler, these were training fields for the much larger elimination he had in mind.

Those who performed these dastardly deeds had to learn to steel themselves from almost any human emotion. They were schooled in how to trick people being led to their deaths and not respond to any of the screams, smells, or pleadings of the victims. These trainees were rewarded for their own dehumanization, not only with special privileges, but also with medals.

AUSCHWITZ MEDICAL EXPERIMENTATION

The psychiatrists were not the only doctors anxious for the gruesome practices to continue. There were more than seventy medical research projects conducted by the Nazis between 1939 and 1945 at the Auschwitz extermination camp. Over 200 doctors were involved in operating concentration camps—conducting medical services and research at Auschwitz. The victims of the experimentation were primarily Jews and were considered subhuman by the Nazis. Many types of experiments were performed including pharmacological, genetic, infectious disease, torture, traumatic injury, and surgery.

Especially ghoulish was one Dr. Josef Mengele, known as the Angel of Death. As the new trains arrived at Auschwitz, he would meet every captured person for the selection process. He actually derived some sort of sick pleasure in the power he had to say, "Right!" or "Left!"; this determined who would live—at least temporarily—and who would die. He dressed impeccably in his freshly laundered SS uniform—every pleat and crease an example of perfection. His dark hair was groomed just right, and as he stood there with his snow-white, cotton gloves on and watched the carnage tumble from the cattle cars; he smiled or whistled.

The killing and the experimentation continued secretly; the pace quickened as time went on. However, despite all their precautions, word eventually leaked out, and protests began to pour in, especially from the church. Something had to be done.

Rather than suspending the program, as many came to believe, the Nazis simply changed procedures. Hitler got credit for ordering an end to the killings, when in reality, the killings just took on a different form. Instead of using the gas chambers and crematoria, they used lethal injections or starvation. Eventually, as the Reich became totally indifferent toward human life, special committees were instituted to "relieve" wounded German soldiers from their pain.

THE FINAL SOLUTION

It was the summer of 1941 when Himmler told Hess that the *Führer* had ordered the "final solution" of the Jewish question—all Jews could then be eliminated. Almost immediately after the Nazis gained total power in Germany, the concentration camps opened, beginning with Dachau. The real fruition of the plans of murder on an assembly line basis didn't occur until the extermination camps were established.

The extermination camps were located in Poland, usually in desolate areas, away from any population. Their purpose was to kill Jews quickly and efficiently. The SS ran the death camps with brutality and compassionless ease. These were Hitler's "final solution" to the Jewish "problem." These facilities were run extremely efficiently with the precision of an assembly line. The Jews were rounded up and squeezed into railroad boxcars like cattle. Then they were herded into the camp and asked to surrender all their valuables for safekeeping. They were then ushered into dressing rooms, where they were stripped, then whipped into the death chambers, and finally gassed.

In some of the more "humane" camps, they were tricked into the gas chambers. These were set up like showers, and the Jews were told they were to take showers and be deloused. When all had entered—men on one side, women and children on the other—the doors were sealed shut, and the gas was turned on.

Afterward, their bodies were pulled out, hosed down, and their mouths were inspected for gold fillings. They were then taken to a crematorium, and later, their bones were ground up and put into sacks along with the ashes, and this was used for fertilizer. Human parts were used to make felt and soap.

When World War II came to a close, Hitler had conquered almost all of Europe. For a few years, from 1942 through 1944, Hitler actually controlled most of the continent. Hitler's failures came mostly in the areas of military strategy, and there were only a few of them. He used every gift at his disposal to the fullest. He took advantage of his great manipulative influence and control over people. He was organized and deceitful, and he had a secretive plan and a thirst for power many say was never quenched.

HITLER'S PSYCHOLOGICAL PROFILE

Hitler viewed himself as invincible. An actual quote from Hitler, as recorded by a British informant, was as follows: "Do you realize that you are in the presence of the greatest German of all time?"

There are many more of these kinds of statements, and there is no question that Hitler believed them. In fact, Hitler believed that he was sent by Providence to lead Germany and to unite Europe under his control. He had no specific plan, but rather listened to an inner voice, which gave him guidance. Thus, he saw himself as a person who could navigate once the voice told him to act. Hitler made the following remarkable statements: "I follow my course with the precision and security of a sleepwalker," and, "But if the voice speaks, then I know the time has come to act."

The first makes no sense without the second. A sleepwalker is not operating with either precision or security, but, if the conscious mind is relaxed, and the individual is following an inner divine voice, that means an entirely different thing. Did Hitler believe that he was acting out of divine appointment? Yes, he did. He stated, "I carry out the commands that Providence has laid upon me."

Hitler was fond of saying how the "voice" had protected him in combat in World War I. He also escaped several well-laid plans for his assassination—forty-two in all—some of which should have easily accomplished the deed; perhaps his "voice" had powers no one was aware of.

There is no question that Hitler's greatest strength was his oration skill. Despite the fact that his own voice was raspy and rose to a shrill falsetto when he became excited, his speeches were spellbinding to many in his audiences. It is safe to say that Hitler would not have had a political career of any substance without this skill. This ability to charm audiences into frenzy gave the propagandists just what they needed. Because of the close, personal connection Hitler made with his listeners, they wanted to believe the best of him. The Nazi press made much of the fact that Hitler loved children and animals, was not a womanizer, and did not eat meat, smoke, or drink. While these were true, one still wonders about this man who loved children, yet sent over 1.5 million of them to their deaths.

ANOTHER HITLER

As might be expected, the real Hitler—who his associates knew—and the one presented to the German people by Nazi propaganda were often quite different. However, there was an interesting quirk: For brief periods of time, Hitler actually acted and looked like the man his propaganda machine had invented. He was brave, clear-headed, humorous, seemingly at ease with people, and he had great insights into complex problems. His knowledge of more or less trivial military matters often astounded his staff. He seemed to know intuitively many factors that relate to group psychology. Some of these are mentioned in *Mein Kampf,* so he obviously was aware of them at a fairly young age. He certainly understood the spiritual hunger of the masses and how to appease it. He recognized the role that women and youth play in these matters and catered particularly to them.

At first American intelligence—the Office of Strategic Services, or OSS—contemplated assassinating Hitler and compiled a dossier that contained many useful facts concerning the private Hitler, the one not known to most of Germany. His weaknesses were also well known by his close associates. Hitler was unable to keep any kind of a work schedule and was almost always late. He slept badly and would keep staff members up to all hours just to have someone to talk to. His mind wandered. He procrastinated, and when his staff pushed too hard, he would fly into rages. Some of these ended up with Hitler rolling on the floor, chewing the carpet, and foaming at the mouth.

Hitler's staff and close associates preferred to ignore Hitler's obvious weaknesses and wait for those few, shining moments when he was actually *Mein Führer.* In between those moments, he was a very troubled little man who appeared to many as a little boy who had lost his mommy. In fact, throughout much of his adult life, Hitler had a close female associate who was much older than he was and filled the role of surrogate mother.

THE REAL FUHRER

Most analyses of this nature assume that the subject's early childhood and formative years made the adult. In Hitler's case, this is not totally true. His early family life looks like some type of bizarre soap opera of Austrian peasants rather than the almost idyllic setting Hitler put forth. It seems Hitler worked hard to get over his dysfunctional family and his somewhat abusive childhood.

Hitler kept details concerning his background from even his closest associates, and he was wise to do so. Multiple marriages, children born out of wedlock, intermarriage between relatives, imbeciles hidden in upstairs rooms, and the very possibility that Hitler was one-quarter Jewish were facts that Hitler wished to bury and ignore. After all, how would this look to the masses? Here was a superman, trying to clean up the race, and he and his family represented exactly what he was trying to eradicate.

Several pertinent facts stand out from an analysis of Hitler's youth. His mother doted on him, but his father was a vicious drinker who severely beat Adolf and other family members when drunk.

Hitler had no problem with Jews until after he moved to Vienna and listened to the anti-Semitic speeches of the mayor, Karl Lueger. Hitler's doctor and several of his associates were Jews, and Hitler did business with Jewish merchants who displayed his art. So how did this ambitionless, amoral young man go from being an Austrian art bum and petty criminal to leader of Germany? The only answer is his innate knowledge of group psychology, his showmanship, and his superb oration skills—and, of course, that inner voice.

THE EXPERTS SPEAK

The OSS reached the conclusion that Hitler's driving force was that he transferred his strong love for his now-dead mother to his adopted country, Germany. It is significant that although most Germans refer to Germany as the fatherland, almost all of Hitler's speeches and writings call Germany the motherland.

The OSS report concluded that, from a psychological point of view, Hitler was trying to solve his personal conflicts and rectify the injustices of his childhood. Unfortunately, he was in a position to act this scenario out on a national level. A war gave Hitler the chance to prove his manhood to his symbolic mother, Germany. He was happy in the army in World War I. After learning of Germany's defeat, Hitler was temporarily blinded, which he attributed to mustard gas, but the blindness was actually caused by hysteria, according to the doctor who treated him.

It was while he was recovering in the hospital from blindness that he started to envision himself as the leader who would make Germany great again. This was reinforced by the notion that the inner voice had saved him from death several times on the battlefield. Providence, he reasoned, must have ordained him for great things, or he could not have survived the front lines. His belief in divine intervention in his life led directly to a messiah complex.

There he was—the savior of Germany, who couldn't be killed by his enemies. This helps explain Hitler's extreme bravery on certain occasions and lack of the same on others. When he was fighting for Germany, he was the supreme *Führer,* and when he wasn't, he was a confused little boy.

DELVING DEEPER

A further support for this theory was Hitler's sex life, or rather, his lack of one. He loved pornography, which avoids all human contact. He liked much older women who would mother him, and he permitted them indulgences for which he would have executed anyone else. They were clearly mother figures, and it is believed that these were non-sexual relationships.

The American OSS intelligence paper on Hitler's psychological profile discusses eight possible scenarios for his future behavior. These were written during World War II, and each area was explored in some depth. The report then comments on the concept of suicide:

> This (suicide) is the most plausible outcome. Not only has he frequently threatened to commit suicide, but from what we know of his psychology it is the most likely possibility. It is probably true that he has an inordinate fear of death, but being an hysteric he could undoubtedly screw himself up into the super-man character and perform the deed.

And as we now know, in the end, this was the avenue Hitler chose.

PHILOSOPHICAL INFLUENCES ON HITLER

Marx and Engels are not the only sources of European thought for the German school of philosophy. For the truly obsessed, there is always Friedrich Nietzsche. In his book, ominously entitled *The Antichrist*, Nietzsche stresses the need for a superman as well as denigrates the common man. Christianity is false because it helps the weak, common man at the expense of the superman and his friends. The superman creates his own rules, and these are the new morality. Love, in the Christian sense, is a means for the commoner to overcome his miserable life. Like Marx, Nietzsche finds that religion is the opiate of the people—and not a very effective one. He recommends Buddhism for at least being more honest, but there isn't really much hope on this earth for the non-superman.

Unfortunately, Nietzsche had a particular hold on people such as Hitler, perhaps because he said what they wanted to hear. While this philosopher would not rate a mention among the great thinkers of our times, his claim on immortality is in those who actually believed him and acted upon his words—not for the clarity of his thought.

DARWIN'S INFLUENCE

Another philosopher whose work we are all familiar with had a deep effect on Hitler. Charles Darwin, of evolution fame, was actually a philosopher as well as a naturalist. In fact, social Darwinism is the most direct route from the written page to Hitler's brain, and then to the Holocaust.

Unfortunately, Darwin wrote *The Descent of Man*, which explained how man is governed by the same evolutionary rules as animals. In doing so, he invariably had to open the door to what others would expound on later.

Thus the weak members of civilized societies propagate their kind. No one who has attended to the breeding of domestic animals will doubt that this will be highly injurious to the race of man. Hardly anyone is so ignorant as to allow his worst animals to breed.

While most are aware of the horrors of Hitler's death camps, few understand the philosophy that undergirded the Nazi regime is alive and well today in a form that appears to be quite innocent. In 1859 when Charles Darwin wrote his most influential book, *Origin of the Species,* most of western secular thought embraced creationism or the Bible story of man's origin. After that many intellectuals embraced the theory of evolution with its "survival of the fittest" concept. But along with that message comes an equally powerful thought. If man evolved from lower species, observation indicated that some groups were further along the evolution trail than others.

Francis Galton was a half cousin of Darwin, and, taking his work, he ran it to its logical conclusion and invented what became the false science of eugenics. As with livestock, by selective breeding, you could improve the human race. Of course it was equally logical that reproduction among the less desirable elements should be curtailed. While Darwin had hinted at such a conclusion in his books, Galton published his work in 1883, *Inquiries Into Human Facility,* and spelled out the concept of eugenics in detail.

NEW AGE BECOMES A FACTOR

Meanwhile the Theosophical Society was founded in 1875 by Helena Blavatsky. Madame Blavatsky was a prolific writer and one of her books, *The Secret Doctrine,* spelled out her version of how the human race had developed. As in Galton's thinking, Blavatsky saw evolution as correct, but it came in racial waves. The last and most advanced was the Aryan race. This group was so advanced that with the proper help from supernatural beings, they could become gods. Thus, what Darwin started and Galton improved upon had now become a religion as well as a philosophy.

In the 1930s, Alice Bailey, a protégé of Blavatsky, wrote many additional works concerning theosophy and wisely changed its name to something more appealing and up to date, New Age. Both Bailey and Blavatsky writings were rooted in the second century Gnostic cult of Christianity, which stated that only insiders with special knowledge could understand these mysteries and with the help of supernatural beings could become gods themselves.

Thus, the underlying philosophy of Nazism, the concept of Germans as the Aryan or master race, lead directly to the Holocaust. It flowed from Darwin, Galton, and Blavatsky's writings and lives today under Alice Bailey's nomenclature of New Ageism.

HITLER AND THE OCCULT

A little-known fact is that while Hitler was raised Catholic, as an adult he turned away from that faith and turned to the occult. It was 1909 when Hitler, barely twenty years old, came across an occult anti-Semitic magazine. He soon became friends with its originators. Lanz, one of the publishers, later claimed credit for being an influence on Nazi ideologies. Both Lanz and his partner, List, were completely immersed in topics concerning blood purity, grail legends, Judaism and, of all things, a New World Order. They also borrowed the symbol of the swastika from Hinduism.

It seems that human nature requires a certain number of secret societies to appeal to those among us who seek out such organizations. They range from the relatively innocent to the violent. In America many college students are drawn to Greek fraternities with secret rituals, which on the whole seems like a good thing. Younger members are mentored by the older members and grades, sports, and proper dress and behavior are stressed.

However, America is also the origin of secretive groups like the Ku Klux Klan (KKK). The history of this organization has been largely one of violence, fear, and intimidation. African/Americans, Catholics, Jews, and immigrants made their hate list. They followed a creed that essentially said the white race was superior and these other groups were polluting America. As many law enforcement personnel were members in its beginning, those who were persecuted did not often see justice.

Like America, Germany had its share of secret societies, some of which did not seem greatly different than the KKK. Several prominent secret societies became quite popular in post WWI intellectual circles. They included the Vril Society. When Hitler was imprisoned in Landsberg Prison after his failed takeover of the Bavarian government, he came into contact with Karl Haushofer, a key member of the Vril organization. He initiated Hitler into this group, which required as a condition for membership a knowledge of Madame Blavatsky's book *The Secret Doctrine*. Haushofer became one of the earliest members of Hitler's soon-to-be-named Nazi party (Let Us Reason Ministries 2009, 1).

THEOSOPHY, THULE AND NEW AGE

From accounts of Hitler's years as a struggling artist in Vienna, it is common knowledge that he had a strong interest in the occult and that he was an avid reader. Prison allows for much reading time, and it is highly likely that Hitler read *The Secret Doctrine* in great detail.

Furthermore the Nazi high priesthood was composed of ardent theosophists and included Hitler, Himmler, Rahn, Rosenberg, Hess, Feder and Sebot (Wikipedia 2010, 7). Many of these were also members of another theosophical group, the Thule Society. Pat Robertson, in his book *The New World Order,* states that members of the Thule Society referred to themselves "as the founders of *die neue Zeit,* the New Age, and they promised themselves a thousand year reign" (Robertson 1991, 170).

Dietrich Eckart was the main figure of the Thule Society and considered himself the mentor of Adolf Hitler. According to Werner Maser, "Eckart's influence on Hitler's intellectual and social development up until the time he wrote *Mein Kampf,* (which Hitler dedicated to Eckart) cannot be overrated" (Maser 1975, 126).

INFLUENCED BY BLAVATSKY

Further evidence of the influence of theosophy or New Age is found in comments Hitler repeated in his many speeches of Blavatsky's doctrines of the master race or Aryans. The Aryans, according to Blavatsky in *The Secret Doctrine,* had "superior intelligence" over the other surviving races. Hitler repeatedly told the

German people that they were the Aryan race. This philosophy often leads to the so-called "science" of eugenics (racial cleansing through birth control, isolation, and castration) and ultimately to genocide as practiced by Hitler in the concentration camps.

Hitler continued in his pursuit of the occult, and by age twenty-nine, he was convinced that he heard voices proclaiming that he was chosen by God to be the German messiah. He later claimed to have made contact with an "ascended master" known as Lucifer. Others eventually joined Hitler and Lucifer as they began to build the Third Reich based on the same principles that the New Age is based on today. Hitler surrounded himself with those of like mind—Himmler and Hess—who may have been, among others, his spiritual mentors.

Hermann Rauschning was an associate of Adolf Hitler's (who defected to the Allies in 1939). He was the Nazi president of the Danzig Senate, in which he recorded statements made by Hitler, which Rauschning says are unintelligible except from a New Age perspective (Anglebert 1975, 178). The fact that the Rauschning book included quotes that he admitted he did not understand only adds to the credibility of his testimony, for these often turn out to be occult references of the kind meant to be understood by fellow initiates alone.

THE OCCULT WAS OVERLOOKED

It seems amazing that so many have dismissed or overlooked this important link to comprehending the Nazi mentality. The Office of Strategic Services (OSS) was the World War II intelligence agency that collected data concerning Hitler. While much of their work was comprehensive and accurate (such as predicting Hitler's suicide) they totally missed the occult connection that drove his thinking. Instead they focused on Freudian analysis, which fails to explain Hitler's campaign to exterminate the Jews and other "unfit" groups.

It is now clear that many who studied Hitler during and after the end of the Third Reich simply did not grasp the significance of what must have seemed to them as Nazi psychobabble. They failed to realize Hitler's speech contained many theosophical and occult concepts, which he considered the rationale for his actions. There is no doubt that Hitler believed in, studied, and relied on the occult for supernatural help. His guiding voice of Providence, his uncanny knack for avoiding death, his ability to not only withstand but enjoy ugly scenes of human carnage, his hypnotic powers over an audience, and his despotic hold over a nation seemed impossible without a lot of help—supernatural help.

Many say that Hitler's final act was a fitting tribute to the occult. In Druid circles, committing suicide was a very brave thing to do. Part of the ritual, however, was that it must be done in pairs. This explains the obvious pact between the *Führer* and his new bride, Eva Braun. Other high-ranking Nazis also ended their lives the same way, like Goebbels and Haushfer. The day chosen—April 30—is an important pagan holiday, and many believe it was purposely singled out by Hitler.

PROOF OF THE CONNECTION

There are accounts of Hitler going through some very strange situations where either he was stark raving mad or talking to entities that he, the Nazis, and the New Age believers all view as real and independent beings. "Almost everyone who has written about Hitler has commented on his rages. His behavior is extremely violent–He scolds and shouts and stammers and on some occasions foaming saliva gathers in the corners of his mouth" (Office of Strategic Services 1991–2009, 5).

Rauschning said, when speaking of Hitler, "One cannot help but think of him as a medium–beyond any doubt Hitler was possessed by forces outside himself–" (Suster 1996, 201).

Hitler berated Christianity for denying "evolutionary laws of survival of the fittest." This is a link to another philosophy previously mentioned: Social Darwinism. Nietzsche, a German philosopher and great influence on Hitler said, "The Christian is but a Jew of more liberal persuasion" (Nietzsche 1895, 195).

The Christian issue, of course, presented an insurmountable problem for the *Führer*. Germany, being a Christian country, required that he tread lightly, so he decided on a partial solution. One that said the Nazis should try to wean Christians from the Jewish-influenced sections of the Bible—most of the Bible—and add pagan meanings to key passages that would help promote their agenda. This idea became part of the 1920 Nazi platform of "Positive Christianity."

New Agers today offer a similar repackaging to unsuspecting Christians. Many Christians actually bought into this new Positive Christianity, but not enough. Hitler made an attempt, prior to his Final Solution, to remove all churches that were resistant to his policies. Leaders of these establishments who would not go along with Hitler's requests or who were very influential and Christian were imprisoned.

While Hitler was busy tearing apart Judaism and, to some extent, Christianity, he extolled the virtues of Eastern religions and philosophies. "Among Eastern religions Hitler described religious leaders such as Confucius, Buddha and Mohammed as providers of spiritual sustenance" (Anglebert 1974, 171). This is just one more tie-in to the New Age Movement, which finds its philosophical basis in Eastern rather than Western thought. Thus, New Agers are quite comfortable with concepts such as reincarnation.

"GROUP THINK"

Two of the main Nazi goals were to erase private thought and conviction as much as possible and to instill a desire for groupthink, whereby the leaders would think for the masses, which needed only to submit. This groupthink was also presented to the SS. It is said these soldiers were expected to be found worthy of their high status and not engage in individualized thinking. They were trained to disregard their emotions and consciences, sometimes by practicing acts of brutality associated with satanic rites. This would numb them to the heinous acts they committed or watched without thinking, but by just following orders.

The "group think" aspect of Nazi training and thought becomes more obvious when examining the seven principles of National Socialism (Nazism). Principle II states:

> We believe that society can function successfully, and therefore happily, only as an organism—the whole thus vastly increasing the power of all cooperating parts, and the parts subordinating a part of their freedom to the whole.
>
> (theneworder.org, "What is National Socialism?" p.1, 2003)

This view is not only popular in New Age today, but it is a central doctrine. Individual human rights must take a backseat to humanity's rights, no matter the cost or pain. Meditation, visualization and a state of altered consciousness, yoga, and Zen Buddhism—all are practices common to both the Third Reich and New Agers.

CHAPTER FIVE:

LIVING PROPHECY

ALL THE BIBLE'S MYSTERIES,
UNFOLDING SECRECY

REVEALED TODAY TO US—
WE'RE LIVING PROPHECY.

Whether they are called neo-Nazis or Muslims, the truth is that we are seeing these same principles of hate and blame directed at the Jewish people all across Europe today, as was once the fodder for the Holocaust of the thirties and forties. There is a startling resurgence of anti-Jewish remarks such as, "Kill the Jews," heard as a chant in Paris at a pro-Palestinian demonstration in January of 2009.

Old Nazi claims that Jews are committing atrocities against Palestinian children are gaining momentum as the anti-Israel media has taken its stand. Scandinavia seems to be feeding on these media reports, and attitudes and sympathies are changing, even among some Christians. London—once a huge Christian city—has become a large base for radical Islam and, as a result, anti-Jewish sentiments.

You would think that New Age and Nazism are no longer a problem since Nazi Germany has long ceased to exist. And it would seem that everyone realizes how stupid Social Darwinism, eugenics, and racial hygiene really are—right? Unfortunately, this is not the case, and it is probably most obvious at its roots in Germany, where neo-Nazism is alive and well.

NAZI MIND-SET

The following paraphrase is from an article entitled "A Gentile's View of Today's Germany," written by a man named William E. Grim in February of 2003 and published on Christianactionforisrael.org. He is American from Ohio, but he lives near Munich, Germany, where he works as a writer.

This man is an American non-Jew who lived where Hitler walked and rose to power, though he had no real connection to these atrocities. While not dwelling on the horrors that were formulated in this quaint Bavarian city, he was taken by surprise when, over time, odd events happened—things like kids on a bus who passed around a copy of *Mein Kampf* and a tape of the speeches of Joseph Goebbels, and all the other kids thinking this was cool. Also, he writes of a business meeting where disparaging remarks were made by four highly educated Germans concerning the Jews. Mr. Grim writes about other times when Germans loosened up in his presence and spoke of things that the world believes died with Adolf Hitler.

He says that he has become quite conscious of anti-Semitism for the first time in his life. He speaks of some of the issues in 2002:

Synagogues have been firebombed, Jewish cemeteries desecrated, and the number one best-selling novel, Martin Walser's *Death of a Critic*, is a thinly-veiled *roman à clef* containing a vicious anti-Semitic attack on Germany's best-known literary critic, Marcel Reich-Ranicki (who is a survivor of both the Warsaw ghetto and Auschwitz). The Free Democrat Party has unofficially adopted anti-Semitism as a campaign tactic to attract Germany's sizable Muslim minority, and German revisionist historians now are beginning to define German perpetration of World War II and the Holocaust not as crimes against humanity, but as early battles (with regrettable but understandable excesses) in the Cold War against communism.

Mr. Grim says that German Jews are asked not to wear anything publicly that might show they are Jews because they might not be safe on the street. He believes that not much has changed since the early days of Adolf Hitler and that the German mindset continues to be a threat.

He goes on to discuss the German support of the Palestinians and even some support for the Arab terrorists who hold anti-Semitic and anti-American views. He hastens to say that all Germans are *not* anti-Semitic, but he believes that anti-Semitism is part of a German much as "Americans are instinctively freedom-loving."

OTHER EVIDENCE OF ANTI-SEMITISM

There are many things going on in present-day Germany that indicate that the Nazi/Aryan mindset is still active. Below is a frightening quote, because music is usually often associated with young minds, and young minds will readily absorb the lyrics and often apply them in their own lives.

"In 2009 German police raided 224 apartments and houses in Stuttgart, Germany, confiscating 45,000 music CDs on a crackdown on music that includes anti-Semitic lyrics. Stuttgart prosecutors reported that 204 people are being investigated for the distribution of the music" (*Sarasota Herald Tribune* 2009, 8A).

This type of showmanship by the government is to convince the world of their opposition to anti-Semitism. But anti-Semitism always begins as an idea, and once that idea is given a voice, it becomes familiar to its listeners. There is a desensitization process that takes place, and eventually, after hearing something enough, it becomes acceptable, routine; and it isn't long before the idea becomes an action. The following quote speaks of targeting Jews by distorting facts and placing blame. The constant rhetoric of "there was no such thing as the Holocaust" is one more example of planting seeds of doubt and hatred.

"Around the world today, there is an increase in anti-Semitism, including hate speech, violence targeting Jews and Jewish institutions, and denial, minimization, and distortion of the facts of the Holocaust. Militant Islamic groups with political power use language suggestive of genocide regarding the State of Israel. The president of Iran declared the Holocaust a 'myth' and said Israel should be 'wiped off the map'" (U.S. Holocaust Memorial Museum 2008, 1).

"History has shown that whenever anti-Semitism has gone unchecked, the persecution of others has been present or not far behind" (Rickman 2008, 1).

GLOBALLY AN ISSUE

From music to politics to government, there seems to be a concerted effort to drive home the point that the Jews are an inferior race that is at the root of all the world's ailments. While it sounds preposterous in this day and age, we know what this propaganda did in Nazi Germany. It is diabolically evil. Yet many seeking answers are quick to latch on to the idea and somehow rationalize it in their own minds. Did the German people really not know anything about the Holocaust?

"Over the last decade, U.S. embassies and consulates have reported an upsurge in anti-Semitism. The rise in anti-Semitism has been documented in the U.S. Department of State's annual 'Country Reports on Human Rights Practices' and its annual 'Report on International Religious Freedom.' This same trend has been reported by concern by other governments, multilateral institutions, and world leaders" (Rickman 2008, 3).

We cannot forget or be talked out of the horror that took place under Hitler's rule. As Christians, as human beings, we must speak up and not be silenced by those power-hungry leaders who want to expand their borders at the expense of God's chosen people. To repeat such a sin on humanity would be unspeakable.

"The story of the [concentration] camps reminds us that evil is real, and must be called by its name and must be confronted. We are reminded that anti-Semitism may begin with words, but rarely stops with words–" (Rickman 2008, 1)

So we can see that anti-Semitism is alive and well globally today. This is a giant step for the cause of the antichrist, who will be able to appeal to the far right (and other groups) with this mindset.

He will be anti-Semitic although his smooth veneer will conceal his ugly ideas and purposes. He will be a "perfected" Hitler.

Had Hitler not been so unstable, emotional and almost schizophrenic, he would have probably been much more successful in reaching his goal. So just how is Satan going to place his man in power, and how will he choose him? First, Satan might review the last attempt to take over Europe—the one by Hitler.

HITLER'S MISTAKES

How close did Hitler come to achieving his goal? Actually, when you view this without prejudice, over time, you have to say he came pretty close. What happened? Where and why did he fail? Examining Hitler's mistakes will shed some light on the whole subject.

CODES AND RADAR

It's always easier to counter an enemy if you know what their plans are. Polish and British code breakers solved the dilemma of the German code sending devices early in the war. The arrogance of Hitler and many of his military men was such that the codes were changed only once and then only because a better code machine was developed. The Allies soon captured one of the new machines and broke the code. Despite repeated advice, much from high-ranking naval personnel, Hitler refused to believe the codes were compromised.

One result was that the otherwise gung-ho Germans became timid concerning their strategy during the Battle of Britain. They thought they must be going up against stronger forces than was the actual case. The combination of codes and radar allowed

Great Britain to hang on when a direct invasion would have overwhelmed them.

PEARL HARBOR

If the Japanese had just continued their steady march across the Pacific, the U.S. would not have entered the war until much later, making Hitler's consolidation of Europe complete.

RUSSIA

As Napoleon could have told Hitler, invading Russia is not a good idea. In fact, history records that few have succeeded. Once again, Hitler would have been able to consolidate his hold over Europe before the U.S. ever entered the war.

WEAPONS

Hitler needed a little more time to develop nuclear weapons, to develop long-range aircraft capable of striking the U.S., and for further development of the jet fighter and bomber. In the end, he could have negotiated a peace with the U.S. that would have allowed him to keep his existing conquests and instead choose to engage in a cold war.

THE JEWISH PROBLEM

Hitler poured too many limited resources into the Holocaust at a time when he could ill afford it. It is very strange to realize, but the very horrors he committed helped to bring him down.

Hitler had most of the attractive features that Satan was looking for in a world dictator, but he also had some rather large flaws. He was so obsessed that sometimes he did not think clearly. He would not and could not think beyond his own fixations. By all accounts, it is not unreasonable to say that Hitler had severe mental defects and was perhaps even clinically insane.

His preoccupation with micromanaging the war is only one indication of a severely disturbed mind. His obsessions sometimes bordered on the bizarre, such as dictating suitable reading matter for his officers at the front. On the one hand, he murdered over 1.5 million children in his camps; on the other, he loved to play with children and genuinely enjoyed them.

A NEW, IMPROVED HITLER

The new Hitler must be a man of greater capabilities than Hitler, since he must be a global leader, but the old standard of hating the Jews will still be a prime requirement of Satan for the antichrist. Satan hates God's chosen people. He must also be strong in both diplomacy and military strategy. He will be polished in the art of speech-making and will say what his audience wants to hear. His true feelings and motives will be cleverly couched—perhaps in Christian terminology, much as Hitler's was—until he feels the moment is right to reveal it. But he must be a perfected Hitler.

Many Germans still think they are the master race and that Jews are inferior and responsible for many of their past or even present failures. Far right parties containing neo-Nazis can be found in state government. Starting in 2006 various groups in Germany have been alarmed at far right gains at the state level. This is especially true in eastern Germany, where unemployment is high and the future for its youth uncertain. The 2006 results meant that neo-Nazi parties were now represented in three of eastern Germany's five states. The far right National Democratic

Party (NPD) has pointed out that they now have representation in a quarter of Germany's sixteen states.

"The country's far right scene is becoming more dangerous, experts say" (Crossland 2009, 1). Jewish groups are extremely concerned about the rise of neo-Nazism, especially youth summer camps that promoted anti-Semitism. The rise of neo-Nazism points directly to the antichrist being of the same mindset as Hitler with perhaps the same or even greater hunger for power.

OTHER CANDIDATES

Germany is the economic and military powerhouse of Europe, and just who would like to face down an aroused Germany—France? You have got to be kidding. In World War II, France mailed it in, and there is nothing now that would indicate any change. Since France has a tendency to bite the hand that feeds them, they can no longer be sure that they would receive help from their "friends."

A French antichrist would have to somehow pacify France's ancient enemy, Germany. There were some French philosophers who seemed up to the German levels of sheer ruthlessness in their day, but that day has passed. The national character of the French people simply does not have the purposefulness to rise to take over the EU. They are not resolute enough nor determined enough, nor do they have the desire to do so. Remember that France was an ally in World War II; as an occupied nation, they understand firsthand the mentality of being enslaved. The lack of power-grabbing treachery in the national character of this nation rules them out as a viable candidate for a hostile world takeover.

From a power point of view, the next likely European candidate would be the United Kingdom. Despite this nation's on-again, off-again flirtation with socialism, the basic underlying philosophies of the British would appear to preclude a British anti-christ—not to mention the problems that the monarchy might present. Once again, the mind-set of the people must be taken into account; it would be inconceivable to the modern Brit to entertain such thoughts of world domination, despotism, and deceit. Their days of colonialism over, that lesson learned, the British are now much more liberal in their political leanings and less tolerant of a regime seeking power over foreign soil. Of course, the fact that they are now only a second-tier nation eliminates even the possibility of dominating the EU, which the antichrist would have to do.

AND TWO MORE

Italy has been suggested in the "guess where the antichrist is from" game, though it's mostly because of Rome being located there. However, Italy is not strong enough militarily, and they are not enough of a major economic power in the EU. Also, it's important to remember that the new, One-World Religion is anything but Roman Catholic. The Vatican would give any Italian leader they didn't care for a tough time.

How about Italy during wartime? Their favorite flag is white, and they'd just as soon invite you home for dinner. Mussolini was a Hitler wannabe whose main claim to fame was that he made the Italian railroads run on time. One of Hitler's mistakes was assuming that Italy would at least fight to protect their own country. Instead, he had to send German troops to hinder Allied advances in Italy.

How about a Russian antichrist? Russia was not a part of the original Roman Empire, and while socialism and fascism are not all that much different, Russia has a different role to play in the end times.

HE WILL COME FROM THE ROMAN EMPIRE

So where will the antichrist come from? As already mentioned, the obvious is often stated—a head of the reborn Roman Empire should be Italian. The Bible does say that the antichrist would be of the same race as those who destroyed the temple in Jerusalem in AD 70 (Daniel 9:26).

However, the Roman Empire was very large in area, composed of many countries, including parts of present-day Germany. Undoubtedly, the soldiers who burned Jerusalem and the temple came from all over the Roman Empire. While in the early days of the Empire, it was considered important to have a high ratio of Romans to others in the Roman Legions, this was relaxed over time.

It is interesting to note that Tim LaHaye, co-writer of the best-selling *Left Behind* series, which is about the end times, writes about the antichrist coming from Romania. Here is an undisputed expert on this subject, and he says that the antichrist need not be Roman and could presumably come from any place in the old Roman Empire. Most experts agree that the antichrist could not be Jewish, based on biblical scripture.

Let us assume that Satan views his best opportunity as one that follows the biblical scenario for an antichrist to head up a reborn Roman Empire. Then, his plan would be exactly in line with the Bible, except, of course, he sees himself the victor in the final battle of Armageddon, defeating the armies of the Lord. His delusions aside, what would be his logical next steps?

THE NEW ROMAN EMPIRE

The Roman Empire reached its greatest size during the reign of the Emperor Trajan. At his death in AD 117, it included about 2.5 million square miles, or over seventy percent the size of the United States. In general, Rome ruled all the lands surrounding the Mediterranean Sea, which they referred to as Mare Nostrum, or "our sea." This territory included present-day France, Luxembourg, Portugal, Spain, most of England and Wales (excluding Scotland and Ireland), and parts of Germany, Belgium, and the Netherlands. Rome ruled that part of present day-Germany that lay to the south and west of the Rhine and Danube Rivers, including Bavaria.

Rome also ruled the land that now comprises Albania, Austria, Bulgaria, Greece, Hungary, Romania, Switzerland, and the former Yugoslavia. In the east, it controlled Turkey, Syria, Lebanon, Israel, and Jordan. In the south, the Roman Empire included northern Egypt, Tunisia, and northern Libya, Algeria, and Morocco. It also controlled the islands of the Mediterranean Sea, and, of course, Italy. The only large, well-populated landmasses not ruled by the Roman Empire were India and China.

The current members of the EU make up most of the western part of the Roman Empire, plus Finland, Sweden, Ireland, Denmark, and Norway. Thus, with the exception of the Scandinavian nations and Ireland, the EU and the western portion of the Roman Empire are very similar. The addition of central and eastern European nations further aligns the Roman Empire with the EU. It seems likely that eventually, almost all European nations will become part of the EU, making it substantially larger than the U.S. economically.

TEN TOES

The ten toes depicted in scripture in Daniel 2:33 tell us that there will eventually be ten dominant members in the EU. This allows for unlimited growth of the other minor members, while the ten would most likely build a joint military force that would be the ten toes of iron. The Bible tells us that the toes are made of clay and iron. Iron symbolizes strength, and clay symbolizes weakness.

The iron is their obvious strength, and most are aware of one inherent weakness in the EU right now. Many of its Member States view this as membership in a trade organization. In other words, they are French first and European second. Or they are Italian first and European second, and so on and so forth. With their loyalty split, it is difficult to act as one. It was not until we all saw ourselves as American that we were truly united. As long as we saw our individual states as separate, they remained so.

Some of the members are more powerful economically, politically, and militarily. Germany is the fourth-largest economy in the world after the United States, Japan, and China. There is no direct comparison that can be made between EU members Malta and Germany except to state that one is strong and the other is much weaker by comparison. This is probably the point that Daniel's vision implies.

HISTORY OFTEN REPEATS ITSELF

So this most important piece of the end-times puzzle as to where the antichrist will come from leaves us with many questions to be answered. What climate would foster and support such schemes? What doctrine would promote expansion and power? Whose history could enable and encourage such ideologies to thrive? What culture would reward an ambition to rule the world? It is not a difficult choice; it's barely a choice at all.

If you look at the period AD 476 through today, who has ruled a united or semi-united Europe for the greatest number of years? The answer is Germanic leaders. This is a fact that has eluded most people. The Germanic Holy Roman Emperors thought of themselves as being in direct succession to those of the Roman Empire. They even called themselves Augustus. Almost all of the Holy Roman Emperors—twenty-eight in all—were crowned in Aachen, Germany, and ruled from that city.

The kingdoms of Charles Martel and Pepin the Short are usually described as French, but both were kings of the Franks, and this covered a territory that includes both present-day Germany and France. Despite the sound of the name, the Franks were a Germanic tribe. Charlemagne, who is sometimes labeled as French, was clearly German, as were the kings of the Holy Roman Empire. From Pepin onward, the European political and military leaders with the most power and influence were Germanic with a single exception—Napoleon.

So, by studying history and taking into account present-day philosophies, and knowing that the antichrist will have to be strong and charismatic with an affinity for peace and the environment, as well as a lust for power and a silver tongue, helps us reach an answer. Adding to this the fact that he must embrace New Ageism, the Nazi philosophy, and rise from the strongest nation in the EU there is only one place he can come from.

FROM WHENCE SHALL HE COME?

The antichrist will come from Germany! There are many other reasons why the antichrist will be German. Perhaps the most convincing one is that Germany has been there and done that and would probably welcome one more chance to be victorious at European domination. There is also the fact that the mind-set of the German people has changed little since World War II.

A new Hitler from Germany would be quite compatible with the worldwide religion—the New Age religion. This is very important because the New Agers will be helpful to the antichrist in his rise to power in both the EU and the UN. The New Agers have thoroughly infiltrated these organizations and are supported by both groups, especially the UN. Those who are part of the New Age inner circle have planned for this moment for a very long time. They have done their job well and are now just waiting for their man to come on the scene.

For Satan, two facts would have to stand out. First, the people of Germany are more conditioned philosophically than any other nation to accept and embrace another Hitler-type leader. Second, any non-Germanic EU dictator would face extreme opposition from the German nation, who would undoubtedly feel that they should be in charge.

Moreover, from Satan's viewpoint, a slightly improved Hitler is all he needs. Why reinvent the wheel when you can go with a proven commodity tweaked slightly to obtain better results?

Therefore, a reasonable expectation is that the world should be looking for a person who is German and will have many of Hitler's characteristics. Like Hitler, the antichrist will come into power in southern Germany. These are convincing reasons that the antichrist will be from Germany; therefore, the antichrist scenario is being built around this fact.

ONE WORLD CURRENCY-CASHLESS SOCIETY

Controlling the world's economic system would certainly be a step in the right direction. Those innocents who will support One-World Government—and there will be quite a few—will also support a one world monetary system. On the surface, it's not a bad idea—no more of those ugly exchange rates and no worrying about whose currency is worth more at any given time. However, Satan's son, the antichrist, has a far more sinister reason for wanting this worldwide system. And according to the Bible, he will get his way—at least for a time.

The debit card is accepted most readily of all our methods of payment, and it would be just a small step to not having to physically carry a card. In Germany, by 2007, it was possible to buy groceries in a supermarket using just your fingerprint. In February 2010, according to Fox News, Colorado police became the first law enforcement agency to use an eye (iris) scanner for identification. In 2009, China's two major leaders called for a new super-sovereign currency to replace the dollar as the major international currency.

Meanwhile, the European Union has already established a common currency that has been accepted by most prominent member nations. So as various forms of monetary transactions are being discussed, we already know, according to the Bible, this will be a cashless world.

HE WAS UNSTABLE

It has been established that Hitler, while relatively uneducated, was an insatiable reader. Much of what he read had a profound impact on him, such as the New Age philosophies and occult articles of which he became so fond. He had delusional visions of conquering the world by sheer will and violence. Anyone who did not agree with him was killed. It is reminiscent of the Queen of Hearts in *Alice in Wonderland,* whose pet line when dealing with dissenters at the most infinitesimal level was, "Off with their heads!"

There was no doubt about it, Hitler was mentally unstable and unbalanced. These are probably two of the major reasons why he lost the war. His obsessions allowed for a warped perspective, and, therefore, decisions based on those perspectives were often wrong. It was amazing that such a character could instill fear into the entire Western world. His instability is what made him so fierce; no one knew what he was capable of doing at any given moment.

Human life was expendable to Hitler. Everything he did was for his own greater good. He was totally self-absorbed, and his delusions became his passions. He believed he had a providential calling to become great. He was a study in contradictions and yet was quite focused on his goal of being the leader of all Europe, if not the entire world; and he didn't care what measures he had to employ to get there.

A COMPARISON

Satan has quite a problem on his hands. He certainly needs a better Hitler, but one who still has many of Hitler's features. Obviously, he needs someone who is likable, even charismatic.

He would be sort of average looking to blend well with the rest of the populace. The antichrist must have Hitler's gift for speaking, convincing and mesmerizing crowds.

He has to be greedy for power and world domination, and he must also possess an ugly mean streak. He must be conscienceless and have an innate lust for self-promotion at any cost. He cannot be squeamish; he will be, in fact, quite ruthless. He will, of course, have the "inner voice," that ability to communicate with supernatural evil forces, only stronger than Hitler since *his* mission will be successful.

As the stage is set for Satan's hero—the antichrist—and given the place in history to which we all have come, there can be no mistake this time. The antichrist needs to possess some qualities that Hitler clearly lacked. He definitely must have more military/diplomatic experience. He should be more educated and therefore more intelligent and articulate than Hitler and have a strong program for peace and the environment. Most importantly he needs to be stable and in control of himself at all times.

PROFILING

The Secret Service's psychological profile of Hitler was so accurate that it correctly predicted his suicide as one of the possible scenarios for Hitler's demise. This lengthy document provided many insights into Hitler's persona that turned out to be quite accurate based on postwar discoveries. Fortunately, the Nazis were great record keepers, and there is virtually nothing that was done in the Third Reich about which we don't have some written information.

Therefore, this profile of the antichrist will be based upon Hitler's psychological profile, additional materials concerning Hitler found after the war, biblical scripture, and some new but logical insights. One underlying assumption has been that throughout the Age of the Gentiles, from AD 70 to 1967, Satan has always had a potential antichrist in mind. At this time, he knows that the rapture could come soon, and he must be ready.

The Bible tells us that there has been more than one antichrist, to which we can all attest. "…It is the last hour; and as you heard that the antichrist is coming, even now many antichrists have come…" (1 John 2:18). However, the final, successful antichrist could be most readily identified as a strong military and political leader from Germany who is able, at least for a time, to unite much of the original Roman Empire.

THE ANTICHRIST

Initially, the antichrist will appear to many in his home country as being a middle-of-the-road politician with good working relationships with both the political right and left. He will be strong on the environment and world peace, thus pleasing the far left and the Green parties. He will also have a strong anti-immigration policy, which will appeal to the far right. Far right leaders will be informed that the antichrist has no love for the Jews and others who supposedly exploit the nation's resources for their own gain.

The antichrist will act as a "tolerant" Christian at first and use all the correct terminology, but in his heart he will embrace the New Age religion. As time goes on, he will show his true colors by denouncing Christianity and blaspheming God. As described in scripture, he will eventually set himself as a god who will be worshiped in the temple during the latter part of the tribulation (Revelation 13:12).

In reality, he will be a cruel man whose true desires will shock and amaze even the most dedicated neo-Nazi. His initial hope will be to rid the world of the unfit or surplus people, as outlined in the philosophy of Social Darwinism and eugenics. He will use the intermingling of the races as an excuse to bolster his argument. This practice, he will insist, has already diluted the master race and polluted the gene pool, thus creating an inferior human. Later, his treachery will escalate until he reaches the point where he will execute anyone who will not worship him.

He will use his deceitful nature by telling the world what they want to hear, at least in the beginning. Later, however, he will set himself up as judge and jury so that any group he deems to be unfit will be strongly persecuted. Eventually, this will be widened to include anyone who will not take his mark. He will be strong in areas where Hitler was weak. He will be a very good politician with strong oratory abilities, but it will be his art of diplomacy and his powers of manipulation—his ability to be a chameleon—that will skyrocket him to gain the trust and admiration of the world.

AS THE BIBLE SEES HIM

What does the Bible say about the antichrist? It says that the antichrist will be boastful and that he will head up an empire that is terrifying and very powerful. It will crush and devour its victims. This kingdom will be different from the others in the past in that it will encompass the whole earth. Thus, we can expect that this will be a worldwide kingdom. Ten kings will report to the antichrist. He will speak against God and oppress all God-fearing people. Three of those kings will ultimately oppose the antichrist, but he will subdue them (Daniel 7:8)

The antichrist will be a stern king and a master of intrigue. He will be very strong but not of his own power—Satan will eventually indwell him. He will cause astounding devastation and will succeed in whatever he does. He will destroy mighty military leaders and holy religious leaders. He will cause deceit to prosper. He will consider himself superior—so superior that he will not be afraid to take on the King of Kings—Jesus—and the heavenly hosts in a final battle. He will be at last destroyed, but not by any human power (Daniel 8:25).

Only once, as told in the Bible, has Satan totally possessed a man, and that was Judas Iscariot. "Then Satan entered Judas, surnamed Iscariot, who was numbered among the twelve" (Luke 22:3). During the first half of the tribulation, Satan will control the antichrist through the inner voice, and during the last forty-two months, he will actually enter the antichrist's body—possibly to raise him from the dead (Revelation 13:3–4). The antichrist will then do anything he pleases, which is really what pleases Satan. He will magnify and exalt himself. He will be very successful in all his plots and schemes, and he will blaspheme God and seemingly get away with it. He will honor a god unknown to his fathers, which seems to be a reference to the New Age religion (Daniel 11:38, 39).

PHYSICALLY SPEAKING

What can we expect the antichrist to look like? The Bible says he will be stern-faced and worship the occult (Daniel

8:23–24). Hitler was described in many ways, and perhaps stern-faced is the best overall description. In general, Hitler was not a very humorous man. Those who recall meeting him for the first time had somewhat different reactions. A few apparently insightful people were appalled at the evil they encountered. Others simply felt that there was something disturbing about his gaze. Some were so mesmerized that they were determined to help him any way they could. A few simply thought he was crazy. A very few thought he seemed very ordinary.

Like Hitler, the antichrist will not have any remarkable physical characteristics; he will maintain a rather low profile until his day arrives, and this is quite important. In Hitler's case, when the time came, it was up to the Nazi propaganda machine to improve on the original. He is said to have worn pads to bulk up his upper body and to avoid the traditional Bavarian mode of dress, which exposed his underdeveloped legs. He adopted his strange moustache as a way of standing out. Mostly, Hitler's personality and natural ability to speak and captivate millions were his strong suits.

His appearance was more like that of a member of one the unfit groups about which he always railed than a member of a super race or that of a superman. Some found Hitler quite odd-looking and many thought he resembled Charlie Chaplin's *Little Tramp* character. In fact Chaplin made a film in 1938 called *The Great Dictator,* in which he played the role of Hitler. While many said he would run into censorship problems, Chaplin's comment was, "But I was determined to go ahead, for Hitler must be laughed at" (Spartacus 2010, 4).

There are many things that Hitler and the antichrist will have in common. For example, they will share a strong belief in the writings of the followers of Social Darwinism. They will both believe that there is a master race and that the pureblooded Aryan

German is that master race. Like Hitler, the antichrist will believe that he is invincible and capable of accomplishing anything. This will be reinforced by early successes, which will convince the antichrist and his followers that he is indeed a superman as described by Nietzsche in his aptly-named book, *The Antichrist*.

He, too, will follow the leading of an inner voice, which in fact will be Satan. This great supernatural force will be able to guide the antichrist to remarkable decisions that will lead to many quick, unusual successes. Before the antichrist can be definitely identified, he will rise through the political ranks and ultimately become a leader in the EU. He will appear to be an average, promising, young politician on his way up until he assumes this role.

HIS RISE TO POWER

This will be done through legitimate political processes, as was often the case with Hitler. His leadership positions will be a result of his charm and manipulative practices, all peaceably attained.

After he becomes leader of the European Union, the antichrist will use this position to be appointed by the Security Council and elected by the General Assembly to the office of Secretary General of the United Nations. Finally, he will have the leverage to set himself up as the ruler of a true worldwide dictatorship. Although he will be opposed by three strong nations, he will prevail.

How will the antichrist accomplish all this? After the rapture, a minimum of several hundred million true Christians—hopefully there will be more—will be removed from earth. Many of those who remain on Earth will be very disturbed by the rapture.

The antichrist, being a charismatic leader, will reassure them that he has everything under control.

Also, there will be an increase in lawlessness, and society will seem to many to have completely broken down. With the advent of the rapture, most restraints that normally exist on bad behavior will have been removed from the earth. Satan and his demons will have free rein to do as they want. Rogue states and terrorist groups will seem like they will end the world with weapons of mass destruction.

GUARANTEED PEACE

Much of the world's population will be desperate for some type of stability and security, even if it means giving up their national sovereignty. The antichrist will guarantee peace if they will just believe in him. His promise will be enough for most to support him as a benign (and seemingly benevolent) world leader or dictator. The final proof of his identity will be his treaty, as outlined in Daniel 9:27, which will appear to create peace in the Middle East. Of course, this peace will be of short duration, lasting a little over three years. Then, he will begin to demonstrate some of the characteristics described above.

It's no wonder the Bible cautions us again and again about being alert—keeping a watch. Yet, despite the increasing frequency by which the signs of the end times are being evidenced, those who write about it are still viewed with a certain degree of suspicion, both inside and outside of the Christian church. Part of this problem is the fact that many past writers honestly thought that their interpretations of the signs showed the end times to be near—so much so that they got carried away and placed exact dates for the second coming. Of course, these date-setters were eventually proven wrong. In addition, there were those who liked to predict the end of the world. These people often carried their warnings to extreme, shouting from street corners and toting huge signs.

It was Jesus Himself who said that no man could forecast His second coming. The warning of the Lord was in Matthew 24:36: "But of that day and hour no one knows, not even the angels of heaven, but My Father only."

We can, however, know the general time of the second coming (Matthew 24:33). Obviously there is a balance. Somewhere between being a date-setter and totally ignoring the signs of the times is where we should be. Unfortunately, we seem to have two factions in place—one that is screaming that tomorrow is the end of the world, and the other, which swears there is nothing to this prophecy business. Both are wrong.

KNOWLEDGE EXPLOSION

We should surely be aware of the obvious. It is common knowledge that there is some scripture that becomes more apparent with the passage of time. The prophecy, which Daniel made about 2,600 years ago, directly points to this day and age. He stated that there would be a great increase in travel and in the spread of knowledge during the end times; "But you Daniel, shut up the words, and seal the book until the time of the end; many shall run to and fro and knowledge shall increase" (Daniel 12:4).

This was not a prophecy readily understandable in Daniel's time; travel was slow, and knowledge seemed fixed. However, with the passage of centuries and the inventions of things like the computer and the jet airplane, it is not at all difficult to see that we are experiencing a lot of going "to and fro," as Daniel put it, and the increase of knowledge spread by the Internet and satellites is undeniable. What Daniel "sealed up" is now much more obvious to those of us who live today. Daniel was told to seal the book "…until the time of the end…" (Daniel 12:4).

A French economist by the name of Georges Anderla developed a set of statistics that mathematically profiled the growth of knowledge since AD 1. His calculations yielded the fact that knowledge first doubled by the year 1500. The next doubling required 250 years, or six times as fast. By the time Anderla completed his study in 1973, the doubling occurred every six years.

While you may choose to disagree with Anderla's figures, there is no doubt that he correctly identified the exponential knowledge trend, which is probably more important than the actual numbers themselves. Not only does this confirm Daniel's prophesy; it raises questions about our immediate future that only God can answer.

TECHNOLOGY AND THE NOT SO YOUNG

There is certainly no evidence that this trend of accelerating growth in knowledge has slowed since then. Today, with the advent of the knowledge revolution, humans knowledge is estimated by some sources to double every eighteen months. Some futurists are concerned about that period in the near future when new knowledge will replace old knowledge almost instantaneously.

It's one thing for the world to acquire new knowledge at a record pace, but it is quite another to master it. There are two particular medical examples of the results of this knowledge explosion you should consider. The first is the deciphering of the human genome in the year 2000. This gave scientists a vast array of new knowledge concerning the human body. The second is the 2007 report of scientists reprogramming skin cells to act like fetal cells. Both of these developments hold out hope for many break-throughs in medical science. Presumably, this new knowledge could lead to cures for diseases such as Parkinson's and might even lead to a cure for paralysis.

Everyone is in favor of the advancement of science to help cure disease, but when does one reach the balance point? People seem to always desire to cross the line, where they go from healer to creator. Advanced cell technology leads to man creating man, which will not be tolerated by God. The possibilities of mad science running amok are here today, and that's when the world must change drastically or end. The bottom line is that knowledge is increasing at a very rapid pace, and it is surely a fulfillment of prophecy.

RAPTURE OF THE CHURCH

Perhaps one of the most difficult end-time events to pin down scripturally is the rapture of the church. This is the catching up of the Christians, alive on earth, into the heavens to meet Christ (1 Thessalonians 4:17). There is a lot of excitement and a lot of speculation concerning just when it will happen; which is just as it has been since the early church.

Christians believe that it will occur at somewhat different times. There have been friendly debates among various factions, and they have even named the various times as pre-Trib, mid-Trib, and post-Trib—these mean that the rapture will happen before, in the middle of, or after the seven-year period known as the tribulation. It's impossible for any of us to precisely identify this time; the end for many of us alive today will be unknowable until it suddenly occurs. Certainly, younger Christians may wonder if they will die a physical death or be raptured before old age overcomes them.

However, when certain obvious things start to occur—events that are agreed upon in both the secular world and the Christian church—it seems useful to examine the facts and see what can be gathered from them. In choosing not to take the comfortable, middle of the road position, by studying some of the signs to which Jesus referred, certain general conclusions about the timing of the end times and specific events may be reached.

Rapture is not a word found in the Bible; rather, it comes from Latin and means "a catching up." There have been others in the distant past who have been caught up, as recorded in the Bible, meaning that they went straight to heaven while alive—they never died.

IT'S HAPPENED BEFORE

Hebrews 11:5 discusses Enoch: "By faith Enoch was taken away so that he did not see death, and was not found, because God had taken him, for before he was taken he had this testimony, that he pleased God."

In 2 Kings 2:11 there is the account of Elijah: "Then it happened, as they continued on and talked, that suddenly a chariot of fire appeared with horses of fire, and separated the two of them; and Elijah went up by a whirlwind into heaven." Verse twelve begins, "And Elisha saw it ..."

These two men were taken up to heaven in human form, just as many will be during the rapture; this is not to be confused with the second coming, which takes place later. Thus there are at least two biblical precedents for God taking His special children directly up to heaven.

There are also other recorded warnings made by the Lord to save His people from certain death. Noah and Abraham's nephew Lot were warned of impending doom. Noah began building an ark long before the flood. In the New Testament, Peter was rescued from prison by an angel. What did all these people have in common? They obeyed! We are told to be ready: "Therefore you also be ready, for the Son of Man is coming at an hour you do not expect" (Matthew 24:44, NJKV). We Christians, too, must obey and be ready.

WHY THE RAPTURE?

There are several reasons why God's children will be raptured. First, thousands of years ago, the Lord made a promise to Abraham: "…And in your seed all the nations of the earth shall be blessed; because Abraham obeyed My voice…" (Genesis 26:4–5). This promise is one of the reasons for God to rescue Abraham's seed, even those who follow him by faith—Christians. As the beast—the antichrist—takes over the world, he will kill all who refuse to worship him. The rapture is God's way of keeping his promise to Abraham.

God also wants to protect His own from torment and wrath. Revelation 3:10 says: "Because you have kept My command to persevere, I will also keep you from the hour of trial which shall come upon the whole world, to test those who dwell on the earth."

Some think this is a good scripture to prove pre-Trib. At the very least, it may refer to not having many Christians on Earth when they are made to take the mark of the beast or be martyred.

God calls us the "salt of the earth," and salt does two things. First, it adds flavor; we add salt to food to make it more tasty. But the more important job of salt, in this particular application, is as a preservative; as such, it keeps things fresh. Foods like ham, especially before refrigeration, would spoil very quickly without salt. By taking the salt—true Christians—out of the earth via the rapture, the earth can also spoil quickly. Without Christians, the world will be filled with unforgiven sin and will allow the antichrist to do his evil almost without opposition.

At the time of the rapture, the dead in Christ shall rise first—that is those whose bodies lie in the ground. Then, "in a twinkling of an eye," those alive in Christ will be caught up in the air to meet Christ. This will leave an unbelievable hole in the world's population. The Bible describes it this way: "Then two men will be in the field: one will be taken and the other left. Two women will be grinding at the mill: one will be taken and the other left" (Matthew 24:40–41).

At a time when we least expect it, Christ will come for His church. Because so many people will disappear at once, many have wondered how the antichrist will explain this phenomenon. As you know, the New Age religion already has a plan in place. The seed is now being planted that Jews and Christians alike pose a terrible threat to the world with their warped, intolerant view of God. So as not to corrupt the earth and ruin the plan, Christians will be ejected and disappear into oblivion.

WHO IS THE UNHOLY TRINITY?

The Rapture will remove everything that now stands in the way of the antichrist's deception and rise to power. The antichrist will have plenty of help in his ascent to dictatorship of the world. Hell itself, with all its ferocity, will be behind him. Make no mistake—this is a formidable force. Without the help of God, humans would not stand a chance against it. As God is good and love personified, so Satan is evil and hate personified. While we should not dwell on the devil's powers, we should not underestimate them either. As fragile as we are, we need to stay close to God and know our enemy.

The Bible calls Satan many things: the destroyer, the accuser of the brethren, the father of lies, the enemy, and the deceiver. It says that he prowls "…about like a roaring lion seeking whom he may devour" (1 Peter 5:8).

Satan has no ability to create anything, so he copies God. This entire last stand of his mimics the Holy Trinity and God—he is the father, the antichrist his son, and the false prophet is the unholy spirit. The Bible strongly indicates that Satan will indwell the antichrist. Revelation 20:2 identifies the dragon as being Satan. Revelation 13:4–5 states that the dragon gave authority to the beast or antichrist and that no one could make war with the beast.

Satan has waited for a very a long time for these days that lie just ahead. Even though he knows the Bible, he thinks he can change his destiny, so he has spent the centuries formulating his plan to totally take over the world. He is no fool! He has considered and reconsidered every tiny detail. He has measured his past failures very carefully and has made sure they will not happen again. His pride is so great that he actually believes he can defeat God and rule his creation.

THE SECOND BEAST

"Then I saw another beast coming up out of the earth, he had two horns like a lamb and spoke like a dragon" (Revelation 13:11).

This beast is like the first beast—the antichrist—in character, nature, and power. This is the false prophet and the one who points to the antichrist and exalts him and calls him God. He has two horns, which shows that he has less power than the first beast, who has seven. He will have a soft and pleasant side "like a lamb," which makes him seem Christ-like. Both the false prophet and the antichrist will look and sound good and will therefore deceive many. "He spoke like a dragon" indicates that he will speak with the manner of Satan and will command authority. He will also speak blasphemy that is couched in seduction and deceit.

He will be persuasive and charismatic and will fool many, even some Christians. His religion will be a false one, like the rest of him, but not many will recognize it. Working with the antichrist, they will be able to seem almost Christian, and only those who really know God will be able to tell the difference.

He will perform miracles and will speak comforting words that the throngs will want to hear. He will bring a convincing message in which the world will get lost. People will be sure he is God. The false prophet will act as the public relations man for the antichrist. He will brag about his expertise, courage, and fortitude, and his words and cunning will catapult the antichrist to world domination.

ONE-WORLD RELIGION

The false prophet suggests worshiping the first beast and that a graven image be made of their new god, the antichrist (Revelation 13:14–15). When it is made, it is the false prophet who gives the idol life and will tell the world to bow down to the image. Those who will not bow down will be killed.

The false prophet will bring the world's population under one religion, which will eventually be worshiping Satan. This will take place halfway through the tribulation (forty-two months after its inception). However, initially it will be disguised as New Age, which will embrace every religion other than Christianity and Judaism. The false prophet will also convince the masses to take the mark of the beast and will thereby control the total economy. One-World Government, One-World Religion, and the one world economy equal a one world dictator on the earth.

Christians and Jews are going to become expendable in the days ahead, and New Age will rise to the top. This religion misleadingly states world peace as its goal. The leader of this worldwide religion, eventually the false prophet, will probably be a prominent religious leader from the Middle East—from ancient Assyria or Iraq or Iran. There will need to be a strong Arab connection since much of the end times action takes place there. Little will be known of his past. However, the key to world peace will be the Middle East.

THE SON OF PERDITION

There is actually quite a parallel between the antichrist and Jesus Christ. We have been examining the unholy trinity and can see how it was copied from God's power structure, but there are other similarities that bear mentioning. Jesus shall rule the world, and the antichrist will rule the world for a time. Jesus performed great signs and wonders, and the antichrist will also appear to cause miracles to occur. Jesus was killed and was resurrected, and so the antichrist will also appear to die and be resurrected. The saints of God are sealed with the Holy Spirit, while the followers of the antichrist shall be sealed with the mark of the beast. Both Jesus and the antichrist have millions who follow them.

There are also definite differences between the antichrist and Jesus. One, of course, is all truth, all good, and all love; the antichrist is the total opposite. One brings life and light, and the other brings darkness and death. One is the real thing, and the antichrist is a counterfeit.

Today, the overwhelming question for us all is the arrival of the antichrist. Is he alive today? How will we know him? When a strong leader arises out of Europe and signs a seven-year treaty with Israel, allowing them to rebuild the temple, Christians will then know with certainty that he is on the scene. Then, some rather specific timing answers will be able to be drawn concerning the situation. If all the facts surrounding it fit the scripture, everyone will know just how close the revealing of the antichrist is, if Christians are still here at all. Then, the task simply becomes to spread this useful knowledge to all who will listen.

Let's look at some additional facts from the secular world and see how they fit into our end-times scenario. Since Satan knows the Word, he is aware that his time is limited and that his best plan is to place one of his own in charge of the most powerful economic unit on Earth, the European Union—or it may be called the reborn Roman Empire. Then his plan will be exactly as laid out in the Bible. The antichrist will be the head of the European Union and eventually inhabited by Satan and, with the support of the false prophet, will bring the whole world under his sway.

This plan must involve a great leader who can truly unite Europe. This is a key in his ultimate world domination. As we know, Hitler, out of all who tried, was the most successful. It is time for Satan to reevaluate his plans, taking the successful elements of Hitler's regime and eliminating the mistakes. Since Satan knows what the scripture says about the tribulation, and since it appears that signs put us relatively close time-wise, certain assumptions can be made that tie this position into the end times.

A LITTLE RECAP

Many Americans don't realize that there is a European Parliament and a President of the European Union. There is a court system in place, and of course they have their own currency—the Euro. At times, the Euro has had a good deal of strength against the U.S. dollar, which shows the underlying economic power of this bloc of nations. Most of the old national currencies have been retired.

Naturally, as membership in the European Union increases, the larger, stronger nations will assume leadership roles. Daniel 2:41–43 says that these nations will give their power and strength to the antichrist. They will be the ten most important nations in the EU and are represented by the ten toes in Daniel's interpretation of King Nebuchadnezzar's dream. They will probably join together to develop a European military force.

With this structure in place, it is not hard to imagine a situation in which a strong leader could emerge and seize control of the EU. How could this happen? Right now, the leader of the EU serves as President for six months and then steps down. What if a charismatic leader, representing a nation that has the biggest economy and most effective military machine, were to decide not to step down? Of course, there is also the possibility that the rules may change down the road, and perhaps six months will not be the standard—more like several years. Perhaps some of the larger nations might unite to oppose this takeover, while the other smaller countries stay on the sidelines to see who will win. Can't you see an improved Adolf Hitler pulling off such a brazen coup? The Bible suggests just such a series of events in Daniel 7:7–8.

AN ATTITUDE PROBLEM

Unlike in the U.S., most Europeans, including Germans, are quite familiar with their nation's history and are proud of it. To a German, it would seem natural that Germany should rule Europe, if for no other reason than that they have done so historically. Germanic tribes sacked Rome. The German chief Odoacer deposed the final Roman Emperor Romulus in AD 476. German chieftains and their people began carving kingdoms out of the provinces of the Empire. The Holy Roman Empire was a conglomeration of lands in western and central Europe that lasted from AD 962–1806, almost a millennium. With few exceptions, Germanic kings ruled with the consent of the Pope. In short,

Germany thinks it should rule Europe, and, as far as they are concerned, history supports this claim.

Today in the EU, Germany has a tremendous amount of power; in Parliament, they currently hold the largest number of seats. Germany can effectively block most EU legislation, not only because they have the most votes, but because Germany is and always has been a most intimidating nation. They do not back away from any fight and the two World Wars were proof of that. They are not only powerful as a European nation, but they have a stern, disciplined attitude and reputation that makes it most unpleasant to disagree with them. Germany has always had the attitude that says, "I should be in charge here."

Some German authorities seem to be under the impression that they have the right to censor the Internet for political content. According to worldfuturefund.org in 2002, "State and regional authorities in Germany regularly police Internet sites that carry political content the authorities consider offensive–Efforts are currently being made to expand these blocking practices from a regional to a national level." It is believed that this case will eventually end up in the German Supreme Court although this may be a decade away (World Future Fund 2003, 1). While this may seem like a good thing since many of these sites are Neo Nazi in nature (pointing out again that the Nazi ideas still flourish), the question remains of how far this could or should be taken.

ALWAYS THE BOSS

On March 28, 2009, German Chancellor Angela Merkel announced the EU needs to "consolidate" before the bloc could take on new members. The one exception was Croatia and on the same day, "…Berlin put the brakes on Montenegro's bid" (Radio Free Europe 2009, 1).

"German Chancellor Angela Merkel said the European Union should aim to create a common army" (Nicola 2001, 1). Of course, the EU member states combined have some 1.9 million soldiers under arms, and NATO, including substantial U.S. troops, is also based in Europe. Why would another army be necessary unless Germany felt they could dominate it?

There are a number of other reasons to believe that the antichrist will be German. The Germanic school of philosophy supports the beliefs of Hitler-types of people, who in turn find sympathetic ears among many, if not most, Germans. While much of Europe today is following the ideas of John Locke and Adam Smith, at least to some degree, the philosophies of Nietzsche, Marx, and Darwin still reign supreme in Germany.

The ideas of John Locke and Adam Smith dealt with economic and personal freedoms and human rights. This contrasts sharply with the writings of Nietzsche, Marx, Darwin and others read in Germany and other places where anti-Semitism and dictatorships seem to dominate. Nietzsche's influence on Nazism in general and Hitler in particular is renowned (Kalish 2004).

These ideologies, with their inherent rationale—that there are surplus, inferior people on Earth, and it is the duty of the master race to eliminate them—can best be described as Satan friendly. These philosophies are familiar to the German people, accepted, and, in some circles, even applauded. They are embedded in the German mind-set and are almost second nature by now; it's like Rome and Catholicism and the U.S. and personal freedom.

DIFFERENT MAN - DIFFERENT MESSAGE

Germany is the largest member of the EU in terms of votes, population, and GDP. Obviously Germany must be placated in all major decisions. This is a much different climate than when Hitler rose to power.

The hyperinflation of the 1920s Germany was followed by the worldwide depression of the 1930s. Germans were sick and tired of economic realities that seemed unrelenting. Hitler was very anti-communist, and many Germans feared a communist take-over, which was very much a threat at the time.

Many Germans also believed the lies that Hitler's propaganda machine spread. Germany needed more land. Germany was winning WWI but was sold out by insider groups, including the Jewish bankers. Germany was in economic problems because of its enemies. Hitler claimed he had all the answers. Hitler promised prosperity at a time when many had none.

So while it is true that bad economic conditions in Germany fostered someone like Hitler becoming a national leader in the 1930s, the better, stronger economy in Germany today will smooth the way for the antichrist. However the antichrist will be a far different man with a far different message. Instead of promising prosperity, he will promote an environmental agenda and promise world peace. And although he will be the same cruel, inhumane leader as Hitler, he will present a far different persona.

GREEN AND PEACE

The antichrist will have a great and viable plan for a green Germany and perhaps even the EU. Germany is a world leader with regard to the environment. In articles in both *Time* and *Newsweek,* "Today, Germany may be the world's greenest country—and not just because salmon once again spawn in the Rhine." And, "Among countries making themselves green by design, Germany is No.1," says Yale's Daniel Esty" (Theil July 7–14, 2008). *Time Magazine* agrees that "Germany's emphasis on renewables has done more than help meet its climate-change goals. It has been an economic success, too" (Blue/Schwandorf April 23, 2008). So we can see why a powerful leader with an environmental agenda would look most attractive to Germans.

The premier job for the coming antichrist is the peace treaty brokered between Israel and the Muslim world and their allies (Daniel 9:27). With the various types of WMDs that have proliferated during the first decade of this century and become available to rogue nation states (and even individual terror groups), the idea of world peace at virtually any cost will seem quite important. "For the Germans, the peaceful balancing of interests with its neighbors and the world has thus become the recipe for success in *European integration,* the importance of which was re-emphasized by the German Presidency of the *Council of the European Union* in the first-half of 2007" (Janning 2010, 2). So peace is of vital importance to the German populace and government.

A person who has a strong but pleasant personality and a great resume with intellectual, military, diplomatic, and political credentials of the highest order will be listened to intently. Much as Hitler's message was that he had all the answers to Germany's economic mess, the antichrist will have a similar message that fits these times and circumstances: "Let me run things, and I will give you a clean environment and world peace."

A few mistakes by Hitler and some bad luck are all that stood between the current European Union and a Germanic-speaking dictatorship. There's no question, though, that Adolf Hitler most closely follows the scriptural references of an evil yet charismatic man who would be able to lie and deceive the masses. Because he ruled over a united Europe, the antichrist will be like him in many ways. He will be stronger, brighter, and more deceptive, as his role will be expanded to world leader, something Hitler only dreamed of.

CHAPTER SIX:

THE TIME LINE

A CENTURY'S THE MARKER SINCE
THE DAWN OF HITLER'S EVIL,

AND IT USHERS IN TERROR AND
WORLDWIDE UPHEAVAL.

According to scripture no man knows the exact date and time of the second coming of Christ (Matthew 24:36). But Jesus said, "So you also, when you see all these things, know that it is near—at the doors!" (Matthew 24:33). In other words, when the signs mentioned by Jesus appear, you know that His second coming is near.

These signs, many of which have taken place, have been explained previously. There have also been many other prophecies already fulfilled, so Christians do not have to be geniuses to say that great things are ready to happen.

Once the tribulation begins, then everyone will know with a high degree of precision when the second coming actually will be. The Bible is quite specific on this point and starts speaking in terms of days during the tribulation and when it will end—eighty-four months after it starts, or Daniel's seventieth week (Daniel 9:27). The sheer passage of time and the actual occurrence of so many of the signs, coupled with some deductive reasoning, embolden us to present a time line for the antichrist that will point to when the second coming may likely occur.

This time line is not a backdoor approach to setting a specific date for the second coming of Jesus. Instead, this scenario suggests a year that many experts on end times will tell you is too far in the future. Many of them believe that the second coming will occur in the first quarter of the twenty-first century, and this suggested year falls beyond that.

A WAKE-UP CALL

If they are right, then our task is even that much more urgent. That task is to inform and alert the unsaved and the nominal Christians that this blessed event may occur before their lifetime is over—that they don't have their entire lives to make up their minds about whether or not they will acknowledge Jesus Christ as Lord and Savior. Most of those who are alive on Earth at the beginning of the tribulation will perish in it (Revelation 6:8).

While there are many legitimate arguments as to whether the rapture will occur before the tribulation, during, or afterward, pre-Trib seems to be the most reasonable. As the time draws nearer, more Christians appear to agree on this. If this is correct, unsaved people will want to seize the opportunity to avoid the tribulation entirely. If the mid-Trib scenario is true, they will want to be saved to avoid the worst part of the tribulation—the second half. If post-Trib is correct, the chances of living through this entire period are quite unlikely. In fact, Jesus states that this period is so bad that if the tribulation were not limited to seven years, no one would live through it (Matthew 24:21–22).

Although there may be opportunities for you, if you are unsaved, to come to Christ in both the first and second halves of the tribulation, chances are that because of panic and extreme pressure, you will follow the crowd and take the mark of the beast. Once you do, you will probably die in one of the many cataclysms that will occur in the tribulation before you have much of a chance to do anything about your salvation; eternity is a very long time to regret your hurried choice.

Thus, by placing years on some critical events in the life of the antichrist, you will see the urgency of the times and that it will serve as a prod to make sure that you have done everything you can to help yourself and others reach the right decision.

BEGINNING THE JOURNEY

A good place to start is at the beginning. Aside from the usual attention seekers, who are able to read just about anything in the tealeaves, all agree that the antichrist cannot be identified by name at this point in time. Why? Well, he is too young, and if he knows his true calling, he will want to maintain a low profile. If he doesn't know the full extent of his participation in end-time events, then there is no reason why he would stand out. It is to Satan's great advantage to keep his protégé under wraps until the appropriate time. If he is to make an appearance on center stage in anything like the time frame suggested, he is alive today.

Also, there are a number of factors that indicate to us there is an outer limit beyond which this time line should not go and still be in synchronization with prophecy in scripture. A key is the 1967 takeover of Jerusalem by the Jews. Scripture clearly states that this date is tied into the second coming.

The second coming could not occur much past one hundred years after 1967 (2067) since it must fall in a period relating to the generation during which Jerusalem was returned to Israel (Luke 21:29–32). Jesus is asked, "…when will these things be?" (Matthew 24:3) The answer is found in verse thirty-four, when Jesus said, "…this generation will by no means pass till all these things take place."

USING THE WORD

Remember the Bible has an extremely high accuracy rate with regard to its fulfilled predictions, although many were unable to correctly interpret the prophecy until it was very near or came to pass. However, 1967 has occurred, and the term "generation" can only be stretched so far.

Several likely possibilities have long since gone with the passage of time. According to Genesis 15:13,16, a generation was one hundred years. Using those numbers, the scenario would pertain to those who were alive and witnessed the Six-Day War of 1967, although the new founding date of Israeli nationhood of 1948 is still a possibility. This would indicate a time span from 2048 to 2067 for Christ's second coming.

Taking into account that no one can identify the antichrist right now and that the second coming should occur by 2067, there are some overall parameters to work with. While the U.S. culture worships youth, even the voters in the U.S. are somewhat reluctant to place an unseasoned person in a position of great responsibility, such as the presidency. Most European countries, including Germany, like to see some heft to their leader's résumé. That heft is not acquired until a person has reached their forties or fifties, and many of our world leaders are older than that. Hitler was forty-four when he became Chancellor of Germany and forty-five when he added the title of president upon Hindenberg's death in 1934.

TWEAKING THE TIMING

This is where a little license is taken in venturing out into unchartered waters. The last chapter of human history is about to be played out on the world's stage. The antichrist is a young man now, and there is almost exactly a century between the birth of Hitler and that of the antichrist.

The premise that a generation is equal to one hundred years is based on several things. First, it is found in Genesis 15:13, 16. In verse 13 God tells Abram that his descendants will be slaves for four hundred years, and in verse 16 He says that they (Abram's descendants) will return in the fourth generation, thus making each generation one hundred years. Also, it seems to fit the signs of the times as we are experiencing them; and it works well with scripture. Satan is a copier and not a creator, and he knows the Bible well. Solomon remarks that "...there is nothing new under the sun" (Ecclesiastes 1:9). That is, things tend to get repeated in history and throughout the Bible.

Jesus was crucified and arose early on the third day. Peter states that "...with the Lord one day is as a thousand years..." (2 Peter 3:8). The second advent of Jesus should resemble the first in some respect since it is such an important event. Early on the third day could easily refer to early in the third millennia after his resurrection in about 32 AD. So, allowing for calendar adjustments, we should expect the second advent no sooner than 2039, allowing for a seven year adjustment. Therefore, using a one hundred year generation for prophesy and viewing the conquest of Jerusalem in 1967 as being an outer limit, the window for the second coming would be between 2039 and 2067. Once again it is certain that no human knows the exact time this will happen, but it will be sudden "as a thief in the night" (2 Peter 2:10).

Therefore, it is reasonable to assume that the antichrist was born in 1989, or one hundred years after Hitler's birth. He was born and raised in Bavaria, the region of Germany where Hitler rose to power. Assuming that Hitler's career and that of the antichrist's will parallel, then this immediately gives us some key dates.

The created time line is what any successful European politician would follow for someone born in 1989. No one graduates from school and announces that he is going to be Chancellor of Germany, or even the Mayor of Munich. It took Hitler over a decade, and some jail time, before he emerged as the leader of a small right-wing party to become the Chancellor of Germany. While his rise was considered quite rapid by some, Hitler worked long and hard during this period. He got to where he wanted to be by rigorously pursuing his goals. There was much planning behind the scenes and many liaisons to be courted. His schedule often included two or three major lengthy speeches and travel in a twenty-four-hour period.

PUTTING A FACE ON THE ANTICHRIST

Alife has been constructed for the antichrist based on the Bible, the facts as they are known, and deductive reasoning. Logic, prophecy, history, and our limited knowledge of psychology have been used to fill in the details and bring this evil man to life. However, although certain liberties have to be taken to build a personality for him, a great attempt has been made not to fictionalize him. The bottom line is that you understand that these events are actually going to take place, and we all need to be properly prepared for them. There are some assumptions that are obvious. For example, no ordinary man can be the antichrist; he would have to have certain beliefs, a total lack of conscience, and special gifts.

Imagine, if you will, a man who possesses an innate need for power at any cost. He will have an ego beyond measure and be inclined to win over millions to his way of thinking through manipulation and false promises. It isn't so far-fetched that the antichrist will be an improved Hitler. The assumption in comparing the two is simply rationalizing that this is the only type of human being that could pull this off.

Our story begins in Bavaria in 1989, at the time of his birth. He has been doted on by his mother but has had a distant relationship with his father. Generally speaking, the antichrist has had a moderate, normal upbringing. He attended school and was a good but not outstanding student. This person is of above average intelligence, but he will excel only in those things in which he is really interested. Thus, his early school record is uneven, and by now he has attended a private military school. The antichrist has gotten a good education there because of his great love for anything structured, requiring much discipline.

After his military academy graduation, he joined the German Army as an officer. The antichrist will serve with distinction and will be considered an expert in military strategy. He will contemplate a military career but will eventually decide that destiny is calling him to another arena—politics. As previously noted, the antichrist will have a great interest in diplomacy and will eventually be a master of it. This will be essential to his rise to dictator of the world. He will win more territory through diplomacy than through military action.

By now, the antichrist has learned to listen to that inner voice, which always seems to have just the right answer, much like Hitler's. He has learned to wait until he hears from it and to do what it says, regardless of how counterintuitive the advice may be. Others notice that he is almost always right, even when it appears initially that he is heading in the wrong direction. The inner voice gives him confidence, and this quality attracts followers.

IN THE NEAR FUTURE

By 2020, the antichrist will have completed his schooling and army service and will actively seek a political opening. He will rise to political power in his home region of Bavaria, and he will be influenced by the philosophies of Darwin, Chamberlin, Nietzsche, and others promoting the master race and the general concepts of Social Darwinism and eugenics. He will be a real star in the New Age arena, once he becomes ruler of the EU, based in occultism, which by then will have grown in numbers to astonishing figures.

While ten years seems like a relatively short period of time, reflect on the changes that Hitler was able to create in Germany in the decade of the 1930s. Germany moved from an economically crippled, Christian nation in 1930 to a powerful warmonger country that attacked neighboring lands without provocation or warning in 1939. Because of the single, inflexible, superior mindset of many Germans, they are easily lead by powerful leaders. His extremely strong and charismatic personality will begin to solidify all the factions, and he will tell them exactly what they want to hear.

To fill in the physical blanks, the following picture has been drawn. He is a fastidious dresser and has a charismatic personality. He will be pleasant to the eyes but not particularly handsome. He will have a high-pitched voice, be unmarried, and have no children. Satan does not want the advice of family members. Thus, the antichrist is asexual and certainly, as the Bible says, he will not have "the desire of women" (Daniel 11:37).

The antichrist will have an intense hatred of Jews. His early exposure to anti-Semitism in Bavaria has been reinforced by his readings of philosophers and New Age thinking will cement these ideologies. This ideology has lead Satan to favor Germans for his puppets in the past, and he sees no reason to change now.

The antichrist will seek out a more conventional route to power. His military connections and innate manipulative abilities will give him entry to a position as military aide to a senior member of the German government—a cabinet-level position. This individual, an elderly man, will gradually surrender more and more of the power of his high office to the antichrist. No one will complain, as everything is running so well—thanks again to that inner voice. While the antichrist will actually learn on the job, his skills will be acknowledged by the few around him who will know what's really going on. The contacts he will make at the highest levels of the German government will prove to be invaluable.

LOOKING BACK

By 1920, Hitler had completed his schooling and his army service and was searching for a new career in Munich. The German Workers' Party changed their name in 1920 to the National Socialist German Workers' Party, which became known as the Nazi Party. Meanwhile, by 1923 Hitler had organized a band of brown-shirted hoodlums known as storm troopers, who were used to fight the Communists or anyone else Hitler told them to fight. He took over the Nazi Party and led a failed revolution to take over the Bavarian government. He was charged with treason but served only nine months of a five-year sentence. He left prison in late 1924. While in jail, Hitler dictated *Mein Kampf.*

A point has been reached now, both in Hitler's life and that of the coming antichrist, where their respective political careers are about to emerge. This is the moment to unveil the time line paralleling Hitler's life to the life of the coming antichrist. Please note the years coincide, with exactly a century between them. Remember that while this is somewhat of a theory as to what will happen, all known facts point to the accuracy of the major points and the general timing.

IT'S NOW TIME FOR THE UNVEILING
AND ALL WILL BE REVEALED.

WHAT ONCE WAS WILL BE AGAIN
EVIL——CLEVERLY CONCEALED.

THE HITLER/ANTICHRIST TIMELINE

HITLER		ANTICHRIST
Hitler is born in small town in Austria near the German border.	1889 / 1989	The antichrist is born in Bavaria.
Hitler serves in German Army until 1919 as courier in WW I. He becomes a corporal and receives German Cross.	1914 / 2014	The antichrist completes education and military service. Works as military attaché to cabinet-level government appointee.
Hitler begins civilian government service as spy for the German Army.	1920 / 2020	The antichrist forms small political party with focus on world peace.
Hitler takes control of small political party renames it National Socialist German Workers' Party (Nazi Party).	1921 / 2021	Economic events favor growth of the antichrist's party's membership.
Hyperinflation destroys German economy; government attempts to pay war reparations backfire. Hitler's attempt to overthrow Bavarian government fails.	1923 / 2023	The antichrist's first attempt at winning a national election fails, but attracts fiercely loyal group of peace activists to his party.

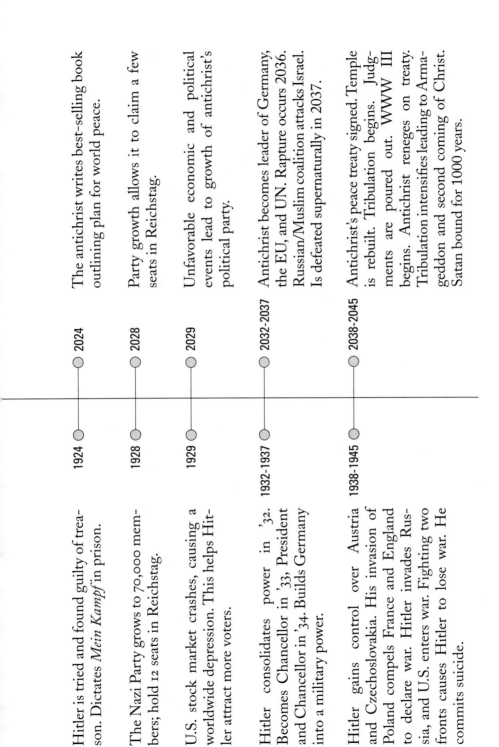

Date	Antichrist	Date	Hitler
2024	The antichrist writes best-selling book outlining plan for world peace.	1924	Hitler is tried and found guilty of treason. Dictates *Mein Kampf* in prison.
2028	Party growth allows it to claim a few seats in Reichstag.	1928	The Nazi Party grows to 70,000 members; hold 12 seats in Reichstag.
2029	Unfavorable economic and political events lead to growth of antichrist's political party.	1929	U.S. stock market crashes, causing a worldwide depression. This helps Hitler attract more voters.
2032-2037	Antichrist becomes leader of Germany, the EU, and UN. Rapture occurs 2036. Russian/Muslim coalition attacks Israel. Is defeated supernaturally in 2037.	1932-1937	Hitler consolidates power in '32. Becomes Chancellor in '33, President and Chancellor in '34. Builds Germany into a military power.
2038-2045	Antichrist's peace treaty signed. Temple is rebuilt. Tribulation begins. Judgments are poured out. WWW III begins. Antichrist reneges on treaty. Tribulation intensifies leading to Armageddon and second coming of Christ. Satan bound for 1000 years.	1938-1945	Hitler gains control over Austria and Czechoslovakia. His invasion of Poland compels France and England to declare war. Hitler invades Russia, and U.S. enters war. Fighting two fronts causes Hitler to lose war. He commits suicide.

A NEW POWER BASE

Liberty has been taken in using a narrative, biographical form so that the enormity of this man's power and deceit and the role he will play in the world's future are made real. While the antichrist will spend about four years as a nominal military aide, he will actually be a powerful behind-the-scenes player in the German government and then will decide it is time to build his own reputation. He will resign and run for a seat in the national government, but he will come off as somewhat arrogant and unfeeling to the voters. His major message of world peace will not resonate well with the German voters he will be wooing; they will be more interested in local jobs and related economic issues. The antichrist will be overconfident. He will not listen to his inner voice, and he will lose the election to a centralist party candidate. He will garner a small but fiercely loyal group of young followers who will be seemingly mesmerized by his vision of world peace.

The antichrist will then return to teach at his military academy and plan to write of his experiences in the German government. Instead, this book will be a road map to world peace. This will become a best-seller and millions of copies will be sold. This will give him an immediate impact on both the national and world scene.

Operating from this new power base, he will form his own political party based on his platform for world peace. He will design a flag to represent himself and set himself apart from other candidates. He will address many international groups on world peace throughout Europe and the world.

PERSONALITY IS KEY

His charismatic personality and pleasant demeanor will captivate millions. It cannot be stated too strongly how important his personality is. His speeches will hypnotize his followers and create in them a frenzy to see this man as their deliverer—as the deliverer of the world! It is during this period that the antichrist will meet scores of influential people who will later help him to achieve his lofty goals.

He will run for national office as a representative of the Peace Party and he will be elected with ease. While his definite plan for world peace will not be spelled out, because he will not yet know what it is, the antichrist will become more and more popular. Polls will show that his popularity is extremely high in France and several other European nations, but his popularity in Germany will not have risen to that level due to his focus on world peace rather than on Germany's specific needs. This parallels the life of Christ, who could gain little support in his hometown and was even almost killed there (Luke 4:29).

Eventually, the antichrist will claim that the solution to world peace is to be found in the Middle East and that he has an undisclosed plan to carry that out. Meanwhile, he and his party will continue to gain strength in the national congress. Up to this point, there will be no evidence that this person is a ruthless, evil tyrant who wishes to subjugate the entire world to his dictatorship. In fact, everything he will do or say will seem to point in exactly the opposite direction. Unlike Hitler, who telegraphed his every move to those who were willing to see the truth, the antichrist will be under the radar as far as his real identity and agenda.

HITLER'S RISE

Meanwhile, back in the twentieth century, Hitler continued his march to national power. The worldwide depression hit Germany hard in 1930, and by 1932, the Nazi Party had forty percent of the vote. Hitler could then block any coalition from forming a government but could not form one himself. In early 1933, Hitler was named Chancellor, and in 1934, Hindenberg died. Hitler then assumed the titles of President and Chancellor.

From 1933 to 1938, Hitler developed a formidable war machine, which was in violation of the Versailles Treaty. In 1938, Austria was absorbed into Germany. He took all of Czechoslovakia in 1939. He invaded Poland in late 1939. Finally, the Allies had enough of Hitler's lies, and Britain and France declared war on Germany, officially starting World War II.

HEADING FOR THE FINISH LINE

In 2032, the antichrist will be ready for his next move. He will pretend to work with the larger centrist parties to hammer out a new government; however, such an alignment will only give him partial control of the nation and not the two high offices he desires. Instead, he will put his followers in the national congress together with a coalition of smaller far right and far left parties. By promising each party specific items they want, he will be able to win their total support as the new Chancellor and President.

In 2033, the German nation will be surprised to find that their government will be in the hands of what appears to be an unstable coalition of groups that basically hate each other. But, by catering to the greed of each party leader, and through his diplomatic skills, the antichrist will be able to develop a workable cabinet, which he will fully control. This shows how clever, cunning, and manipulative the antichrist will be.

By 2034, his Peace Party will make up thirty-three percent of the German national congress, and the antichrist will be ready to become the nation's leader. Economic prosperity in Germany will have allowed the voters to focus more on world issues, and the antichrist will sense that the time for a move is at hand.

Those who will support the antichrist during this period will find that their personal finances have greatly improved, while those who oppose him will seem to have fallen on hard times. The antichrist will use the full resources of the German government to reward and punish as he pleases. While rumors of this surface, the antichrist's obvious popularity among a large but not majority segment of the German electorate, plus his great popularity outside the nation, will cause most Germans to want to at least give him a chance.

WELL ON HIS WAY

Soon, the antichrist will begin to operate on an accelerated time schedule. As undisputed leader of Germany, he will put his natural talents to work to win the world. Despite the fact that the next presidency of the EU was not scheduled to go to Germany, he will charm and cajole his way right into the hearts of the powers that be and have that post offered to him. He will graciously accept with a stirring speech of false humility. At the end of the term period of this office, he will simply announce that he will retain that office on a permanent basis. For the first time, some opposition groups will begin to develop, and rumors will spread that this man may not be all he appears to be.

The antichrist will time his move carefully. The EU military forces will be under the command of a loyal friend from his military academy days. Also, the German forces not committed to the EU will be directly under his command. Those who oppose him will be left to wonder how they could effectively do anything to stop him. There will be no military force in Europe that could successfully oppose the antichrist, at least on paper. The nations who allowed the concept of an EU force to reduce their own nation's military capabilities will suddenly realize the vulnerable spot in which they have put themselves.

The EU member nations will have no choice but to go along with this coup. To avoid any useless bloodshed, a majority of EU members will vote to make the antichrist the permanent President of the Council. Shortly thereafter, he will announce that he will also assume the title of President of the European Parliament, thus consolidating his power. The antichrist will then control all of Europe, including all significant military forces there. The United States will have long since removed all of its military forces in Europe in a budgetary move. After all, who would attack such a militarily powerful organization as the EU?

IT BEGINS TO TAKE SHAPE

From 2033 to 2037, the antichrist will consolidate his power in the EU and then will begin his successful takeover of the UN. The antichrist will become fully aware of the importance that religion will play in his plans. He will already have solidified friendship with the false prophet, a popular Middle Eastern Muslim, who will have declared himself *Caliph* over all Islam.

Scripture concerning the false prophet and antichrist states: "Then I stood on the sand of the sea. And I saw a beast rising up out of the sea..." (Revelation 13:1). This is the antichrist, and he rises from the sea, which means he comes from the Gentiles.

According to Hal Lindsey in his book *Apocalypse Code,* the antichrist rises out of the sea (Revelation 13:1), which is a code symbol later defined in Revelation 17:1, 15. Verse 1 talks about the "...great harlot who sits on many waters." Verse 15 explains that the waters are the "...peoples, multitudes, nations, and tongues." The antichrist thus comes from the chaos of the Gentile nations, likened to a stormy sea. Then, in Revelation 13:11, it says: "...I saw another beast coming up out of the earth..." The earth is Israel because, also according to Lindsay, the original Greek is a reference to land, not earth, and in the Bible the term land always refers to the land of Israel, unless otherwise noted (Lindsay 1997, 184–191).

NOT REALLY A CONTRADICTION

The false prophet coming from Israel is inconsistent with Bible. The term beast was reserved for Israel's worst enemies and would not be used against an Israeli. The Israeli's sharp distinction between man and beast is found in Exodus 22:19, "Whoever lies with an animal shall surely be put to death."

Because "out of the earth" usually means out of Israel, this scripture has proven confusing to most people. How can the false prophet come from Israel or "out of the earth" and still be called a "beast," a term never used for Israelis? This seems like a gross contradiction. But...what if the false prophet does come out of Israel and the Bible means exactly what it says? Suppose, he was actually born in Israel—a Jew who converted to Islam. Thus, he has come from the earth or land. And, taking it a step further, what if the false prophet carefully conceals his true background and develops his own fake resume and biography, murdering anyone who knows the truth or even thinks they do?

As the antichrist's right hand man, the false prophet provides insight and information from both sides, allowing the antichrist to present a well thought out plan for peace, pleasing to all parties. Because the false prophet was born a Jew and is now a Muslim, he understands both sides, and he knows what pushes each one's buttons. This is a decided advantage. The false prophet is a true son of Satan, as treachery and deceit are his strengths. He is greedy and lusts after power and is the perfect partner and mouthpiece for the antichrist.

ISLAM

Up until now, you may have noticed that Islam is strangely absent from this book and most other end-times books. The only other monotheistic religion in the world whose theme was originally taken from the Judeo-Christian writings is Islam. It has corrupted the Bible—they say we corrupted it—and rewritten it as the Koran. The Muslims and the religion of Islam are about to enter center stage. It is important, therefore, to know the history of the present-day conflict between the Arabs and the Jews.

The Bible teaches us that Isaac and Ishmael were half-brothers with a common father, Abraham. Sarah, Abraham's wife, could not conceive and so allowed her Egyptian handmaiden, Hagar, to lie with her husband. This was not the plan God had for Abraham. Sarah came to resent Hagar's haughty behavior, and she began to treat her harshly, so Hagar fled with Ishmael. The sons of Ishmael are the Arab nations, and the Jews are the descendants of Isaac. There will never be a lasting peace between the sons of Ishmael and the sons of Isaac, according to scripture.

The Bible says, "He (Ishmael) shall be a wild man; His hand shall be against every man,... And he shall dwell in the presence of all his brethren" (Genesis 16:12).

Talk about prophecy being fulfilled! Thousands of years ago, God's Word told us there will never be lasting peace in the Middle East. Those who attempt to broker treaties today between these two groups don't understand even a few of the difficulties inherent in such a plan. Their basic belief systems are established on two totally different principles—hate and revenge versus the Ten Commandments. Politically, the Arabs are quite comfortable with a tribal theocracy. The concepts of democracy and individual liberties are quite foreign to them. Also, the Arabs view treaties as an opportunity to gain a strategic advantage over a foe.

HITLER RESURFACES

There is more recent history about the Arabs that is not generally known. There was a relationship between Hitler and the Arab world. Hitler visited the Mufti of Jerusalem in 1939, a fact that was recorded in the newspapers of the time with photos of the two leaders together. The Mufti was and is a top Muslim religious leader in the Islamic world.

Needless to say, Hitler found a very sympathetic audience as he discussed his plans for the elimination of Europe's Jewish population. In fact, the Mufti gave Hitler ideas that he put into use when implementing the Holocaust. These included the use of large cremation ovens, yellow patches to identify all Jews, and several other approaches that appealed to and were used by Hitler. At the Nuremberg Trials, Eichmann's deputy Dieter Wisliceny (subsequently executed for war crimes) testified: "The Mufti was one of the initiators of the systematic extermination of European Jews—I heard him say, accompanied by Eichmann, he had visited incognito—the gas chamber of Auschwitz" (Palestinefacts.org 2010, 1).

This relationship went beyond their mutual discussion of the hatred of Jews. The Mufti was able to provide Muslim recruits for Hitler's armies that amounted to two of Hitler's eight divisions. These personnel were largely recruited from Muslim Croatia and were led by Croats. Not only did the Muslim world actively help with strategies and personnel, but it also helped financially from oil-rich states such as Saudi Arabia.

THE MUFTI CONNECTION

While this was not done on an official basis, captured Nazi records found after the war spell this relationship out in detail. "In Berlin, Husseini (the Mufti) used the money confiscated from Jewish victims to finance pro-Nazi activities and to raise 20,000 Muslim troops in Bosnia" (Bedein 2010, 1).

This is important because the Arab world will play a big part in the end times. Couple that with the fact Germany presently has a strong neo-Nazi movement, which may well be supported by a significant percentage of the German people. Attempts to rewrite recent history in order to downplay the scope of the Holocaust are just one indication of this sad state of affairs.

Obviously, the antichrist will be someone the Arab world would be comfortable with, especially when signing a peace treaty with Israel. The Nazi philosophy fits neatly with that of the Arab world. Islam views treaties as periods of time when they can strengthen themselves and perhaps launch a surprise attack. Hitler did the same with Russia. Take these facts and add an Arab false prophet as the right hand man to the antichrist; mix it all together, and you have the ingredients for World War III.

BACK TO THE FUTURE

The antichrist, who will only be looking for a temporary peace, will use this history to his advantage. He will know when it is time for the peace plan to be fully developed and implemented. He will work well with the false prophet. The antichrist will come up with the following secret peace plan.

Israel and its enemies (primarily Islamic nations) will sign a peace treaty that will give Israel permanent peace and the right to rebuild the temple. The Islamic nations will be granted the permanent headship of a new world religion, and the false prophet will be its leader.

During the tribulation, the antichrist will rely on the public relations of the false prophet to exalt and promote him to the level of a god who should be worshiped. This has always been a goal of Satan's; remember Satan promised Jesus the entire world if He would worship him in Luke 4:6–7. The false prophet will use the New Age philosophy with enough input from Islam to keep the Muslims happy with a one-world religion. New Age will already be a major force around the world. Just after the rapture, there will be very few Christians to object.

So this religion, based upon New Age philosophies, will embrace all religions, cultures, and philosophies except Christianity and Judaism, much as the New Age does today. But not because the New Agers haven't tried to be all-inclusive. At first New Agers will try to convert Christians and Jews. Some Christians will be convinced, but most practicing Jews will not. Thus anti-Semitism will grow, and Christians will be discriminated against.

The New Age will be, in that secular world, inoffensive, very tolerant, and most pliable. People will be able to pick and choose the parts they want and leave the rest. Its aim will be to lull everyone into a false state of security by making it easy and comfortable with very few rules and regulations. The only difference from today's New Age is that it will have some Islamic ideas in it, and a Muslim leader will always be its head. Daniel 11:38 says that the antichrist will honor a god his fathers did not know—in other words, a new religion.

Meanwhile the Jews will be content enough with their new treaty because the majority of the Israel does not actually practice Orthodox Judaism. That is to say, they are civil Jews. It's similar to "Christians" who grew up in the church but don't really "walk the walk" daily. Many Jewish Israelis feel that being Israeli means living among Jews, speaking Hebrew, in Israel. The common thought in Israel today is that there is no need to perform religious observances in order to be "Jewish," which conforms to the predominant Israeli-style civil religion. So this allows for a more generous attitude when it comes to having peace, for this nation that has been war-torn since its inception.

IT ALL UNFOLDS

During 2036 and 2037, two events will occur that will greatly disturb the world's population. First, the rapture will occur in 2036, which will cause several hundred million people to suddenly disappear. This will have several profound effects. It will remove all of the forces for good in the world, including the Holy Ghost. Lawlessness will abound. It will become obvious to everyone that something needs to be done. The general feeling will be that anything that brings a measure of stability would be great.

Second, in 2037, Russia and a coalition of Muslim allies will attack Israel, intending to destroy it. Smith's Bible Dictionary states, "The notices of Magog (region of Gog) lead us to fix a northern location" (p. 375). Hal Lindsay refers to "a time when the Islamic world can draw Russia into an alliance against Israel" (Lindsay 1994, 201). And Ezekiel lists the coalition that Russia leads; among them is Persia, now Iran, and the natural leader of Muslim forces from our modern perspective. God destroys the great army supernaturally (Ezekiel 38:1–9).

"'And it will come to pass at the same time, when Gog [Russia] comes up against the land of Israel,' says the Lord God, 'that My fury will show in my face…Surely in that day there shall be a great earthquake in the land of Israel…I will rain upon him…great hailstones, fire, and brimstone'" (Ezekiel 38:18–19, 22). It's obvious that a defeated Russia with depleted resources, especially militarily speaking, could hardly support the antichrist after their defeat in Israel.

This war will severely weaken the Muslim nations, who will then be left without much of a military force, making it easier for the antichrist to work out the details of a peace treaty with Israel and her Muslim neighbors. While the exact number and makeup of the nations in the anti-Israel coalition is debated by biblical scholars, it seems that the two major players are Russia and Iran, joined by a number of other Islamic countries.

UP STEPS THE ANTICHRIST

It is under these circumstances that the antichrist will promise world peace and an end to instability and will come to be appointed head of the UN. The false prophet—the respected religious leader of the Muslim world—will support the plan as well, and he will have gained great credibility by forecasting the rapture, which he refers to as the "ejection of the wicked." Like Hitler, the antichrist will appear to be very lucky and quite smooth. He will survive several assassination attempts, and good things that will appear impossible will happen. No one will seriously object in the beginning, and the peace plan will be signed and implemented in 2038. The Israelis will immediately rebuild the temple, and the seven-year tribulation will begin.

Step one of the antichrist's world peace plan will be in place. Step two will be to divide the world into ten regions, as outlined in Revelation 13:1, with the leader of the most powerful nation in each region as head (or king) of that region. Both smaller and larger nations will surrender more of their sovereignty to the UN, and the earth will be effectively under One-World Government. Some power will be retained at the regional level, but this will be taken from them later by the antichrist. This plan will appeal to the One-World Government types and the New Agers who will be given an advanced look at the plan.

ALMOST TOO EASY

Many people today wonder how such a thing as Nazi Germany could have taken place in a civilized world. Now that it is about eighty years in the past, we simply excuse the events as an unsophisticated people following a charismatic leader right to hell. We believe what we choose to believe and hear what we want to hear; we believe that it could never happen again—not now, and not with all of our education and technology.

The world is a much smaller place, and for anyone to even intimate that we could be as blind today as they were in the thirties is just ridiculous. Therefore, the idea that a person, even one with all the forces of hell on his side, could dupe an entire nation and then the world is simply ludicrous. So, with this thinking in mind, the antichrist cannot simply be personable enough to step into power and control and fool the entire world.

The fact is that this is more than possible—even probable. From a natural standpoint, this has been repeated throughout history. Being a great orator and having a magnetic personality have often been enough to get the wrong, or in some cases even the right, person in leadership. The point is that it is often the only thing by which we judge a leader.

GREAT ORATORS

The Greeks were the first recorded civilization to study oration and to develop it as an art form. The speeches of Pericles and Aristotle are examined to this day. This gift of speech-making was picked up by Romans such as Cicero, and then by Christians such as Augustine, and later Martin Luther. Against all odds, Great Britain held out against far superior German forces in the Battle of Britain in 1940. Many historians credit the speeches of Winston Churchill for seeing the UK through this almost impossible task.

America has had its share of great orators. Who can forget Patrick Henry's "Give me liberty, or give me death"? Or Lincoln's Gettysburg address, which marked the turning point in the Civil War? Remember FDR telling us on the occasion of his first inauguration in 1933 that "The only thing we have to fear is fear itself"? More importantly, we believed it.

Hitler was perhaps the best example of a man who hypnotized his audience with his speaking, and he used this gift to catapult himself into a godlike status. Evil can often spring from the use of persuasive speech. Numerous Latin American dictators of the last century, who were usually on the wrong side, were great and convincing speakers. People like Juan Peron literally mesmerized the people of Argentina. Fidel Castro never left a Cuban audience wanting more, as he held them enthralled for hours at a time.

People are prone to follow the convincing words of a gifted speaker, especially when times are tough. When looking for answers, the most unlikely men have come to the foreground. This country, for example, has experienced the worst economic times in seventy years recently. We were looking for help, relief, and answers and searching for a savior; someone new, someone different. Who exudes more righteousness and confidence than a relaxed man who is offering solutions and is willing to promote and even lead in the battle for change?

SILVER TONGUED

So it was in 2008 America—we were a nation used to being a leader, used to being wealthy, and used to great freedom when the housing and financial crisis brought down industrial and commercial giants from the arenas of auto manufacturing to banking and real estate. People began to panic; their savings were disappearing before their very eyes, and it was at that moment that elections happened to be taking place. A hitherto unknown superhero stepped onto the stage and hypnotized his audience with speeches of recovery, prosperity, and change.

He became our forty-fourth president, our first black president, our first president with a Muslim lineage, and a president with a very un-presidential-sounding name. He was one of the very few non-military men elected to the office in recent times with almost no significant political experience. When it came to being vetted and opening up his past to the citizens of this great land, he simply said, "No!" And everyone backed off; nosey reporters and angry citizens and curious intellectuals all simply let go of this very important issue.

How could such an unknown, simply by saying what everyone wanted to hear; by comforting and cajoling the worried and the fearful, gain entree to the highest office in the western world? Americans were ready for a change, and he said that magic word and people rallied round his call for "change." So no one can say that a charismatic man with the right message at the right time cannot charm the sophisticated world.

WE CAN BE SWAYED WITH WORDS

Anyone can look at Barack Obama and wonder how much was truth, how much was rhetoric, and whether or not he is capable of doing great things as well as saying them. If he is not, how much damage can he do? These are questions only history will answer, but his very existence as President of the United States proves to us that even today, we can choose an unknown person, convinced that we do know him when we really only know his words.

However, we were willing and perhaps a bit desperate for someone really different. We really were looking for change and real answers, much like the Germans were looking for solutions for their defeat in World War I. Along with an answer to their economic crises; they were willing, perhaps even eager, to give the young, upstart Hitler a crack at putting things right.

So when speaking of the antichrist and his soaring to the top of a world lost in confusion and war it is possible even today to be won over by the right personality at the right time. But there is also a spiritual explanation. It is about what our Creator has called us from the very beginning—sheep.

LOOKING FOR A LEADER

Sheep are followers, and they all need the right shepherd to provide for them. Anyone less than totally committed to this job, and the sheep could starve or be eaten by predators. They are not very bright, have no natural defenses, and they depend completely on their leader—their shepherd. Many a shepherd has led their flock astray, like the Hitlers of the world. Knowing we are followers and knowing we hate to move far from our comfort zones, God has given us Jesus, the Good Shepherd, for us to follow, but many have chosen not to follow him and have gone down roads fraught with danger; they continue to tempt fate.

Put the natural and the supernatural together, and we can all see that we need good leaders. Good leaders are sometimes charismatic but not always. Following someone because he speaks well and often of the same things that trouble our hearts is simply not enough. The ultimate proof of this will be the coming antichrist. We are neither too intelligent nor too sophisticated to know what's in a person's heart. We only know what they are willing to show us and to share with us, and for the majority, unfortunately, that is enough.

CHAPTER SEVEN:

THE ABSOLUTE END

IT'S TIME—THE FINAL HOUR.
DO YOU WIN OR LOSE?

COME PEEK INTO ETERNITY—
WHICH SIDE DO YOU CHOOSE?

The signs of the times, Biblical prophecy, political events and even recent archeological digs are in agreement that the end is near. The changes in climate, natural disasters, and the growth of travel and knowledge all put us in the last days. Many theological experts and believers know in their spirit that the church age is almost over. Jesus said that no one knows the exact date or the hour of His second coming except the Father, but as prophecy after prophecy comes true, it seems that the only conclusion one can draw is that the end of days is near. The only question for most is how near?

Two different methods have been used to calculate a similar timeline—a countdown, if you will, to Armageddon. The first was based on a one hundred year parallel between the rise of the antichrist and the rule of Adolf Hitler. The similarities between these two evil men seem uncanny, so it is only fitting that Satan use his most successful model to produce the real thing, the son of perdition. The second approach is one which we are about to briefly explore and is based on biblical scripture both in the Old and New Testaments. It is a combination of Daniels's and Peter's chronological order of the end times in prophecy.

THE BIBLICAL TIMELINE

In Revelation 12:6, there is reference to the second half of the seven-year tribulation period being 1,260 days. Thus the prophetic year is 360 days—1,260 divided by 3.5 . This should not be too surprising, since many ancient cultures used a 360-day year, including the Hebrew and Roman calendars.

In Daniel's vision of seventy years (Daniel 9:24–27) the nation Israel is the time clock for human history. Daniel references a period of seventy weeks, actually seventy times seven—seven days in a week—or 490 days. Prophetically, each day represents one year. Why? In Numbers 14:34, God punishes the spies and those who believed them, who returned from the promised land with negative reports. He was angry and told them that for each day "…you shall bear your guilt one year…". The forty days of their experience in the promised land translated into forty years of the Jews wandering in the wilderness. Thus, 490 days equals 490 years.

Daniel further specifies that the first seven weeks will be the time the Jews will take to rebuild and restore Jerusalem. During those forty-nine years (seven times seven), from 445 BC to 396 BC, the city of Jerusalem was completely rebuilt.

Rebuilding the city took an inordinate amount of time because surrounding enemies hindered the progress. Persia had defeated the Babylonians and released the Jews in 445 BC after being held in captivity for seventy years (Ezra 1:1–4). This was accurately prophesied by both Daniel and Jeremiah (Daniel 9:1–2, Jeremiah 25:10–12). Thus, it should not be surprising that the rest of the seventy weeks of seven have great meaning.

So once Jerusalem was rebuilt there remained sixty-two sevens until the Anointed One would be "cut off" (Daniel 9:26). This too was fulfilled. When the remaining sixty-two weeks or 434 years is added to when the city was rebuilt, it takes us to the date of AD 32, or the year in which Jesus was crucified. Thus, of the first seventy weeks of years, sixty-nine have been fulfilled. The remaining one week is reserved for the tribulation, or the seven years of rule by the antichrist.

THE CHURCH AGE

Now we must account for the two thousand plus years of the church age. Peter tells us, "…that with the Lord one day is as a thousand years, and a thousand years as one day" (2 Peter 3:8). Jesus returned from the grave very early on the third day. Thus, the church has two days to complete its reign or the period from Pentecost to the beginning of the tribulation. And the second coming might be expected just after the end of the second day, or after two thousand years or when the church age is over.

If Jesus was crucified in AD 32, adding two thousand years and then adding seven more to eliminate errors in calendar adjustments brings us to 2039. Why seven years for calendar adjustments? Experts vary on this but agree that Jesus was born several years earlier than AD 1 as a result of calendar adjustments; and the bright star followed by wise men is said by astronomers to have been in BC 7 according to our current calendar.

Therefore, when the time periods are lined up with our previous antichrist/Hitler timeline, the years closely coincide. Thus, there are two viable approaches that give us just about the same result. One is the conclusion reached by following the signs of the time as Jesus instructs us in Matthew 24:4–15 and filling in with logic based on history. The other is rooted in the text of the Bible. There are many arguments that can be made for or against these timelines, but the point is that Biblical prophecy is not just an esoteric subject for theological study, and should be of great concern to all who live in this time period.

The major message is: Are you ready to be judged by the living God of the Universe? While no one knows the exact time the tribulation will start, you certainly want to avoid living through that final seven-year period. True believers will be caught up into the sky in the rapture and return with Jesus as a conquering army. Most of the people left on Earth will perish in a variety of very unpleasant ways as described in the Book of Revelation.

THE TERRIBLE TRIBULATION

For those who still aren't sure, the remainder of this chapter should be read with care and with a Bible in your lap for verification. There are some symbols used in the Book of Revelation, which, among other things, detail the seven-year tribulation, but most of the descriptions are very clear. There is going to be a huge loss of life during this period—2039 through 2045 by our calculations—but don't forget many experts think it will be sooner. It's going to get progressively worse the further into this period you live. In fact, Jesus warns us that if this tribulation period were not shortened to the seven specified years, there would be no one left alive (Matthew 24:21–22).

Two of the many unpleasant alternate names for this period, aside from the tribulation, were given by the Old Testament prophets. They include "The Overflowing Scourge," in Isaiah 28:15–18, and "A Day of Devastation and Desolation" in Zephaniah 1:15. This will be the greatest period of human suffering ever experienced in the world. Think of it as a worldwide Holocaust. Those who don't suffer under the wrath of God will do so under the wrath of the beast—the antichrist. While the period of time appears short, it certainly will not be for those who are living through it.

Why is this happening? The prophet Daniel tell us, "To make an end of sins, to make reconciliation for iniquity, to bring in everlasting righteousness, to seal up vision and prophesy, and to anoint the Most Holy [Jesus]" (Daniel 9:24). One of the purposes of the tribulation is to force the people of the earth to choose between Christ and antichrist. Regardless of whom they choose, the majority of the people alive during this period will die, either as martyrs for God by the beast, or—if they choose the antichrist—by the wrath of God.

THE PEACE TREATY BEGINS IT

In short, God will not be tolerant of sin forever. While he is gracious, the time is coming when you will not have a second chance; the sooner you decide, the better. Those who don't repent can expect the worst. Either way is probably death, unless you choose God before the rapture. This is not so much about what happens here on the earth during your life; it is more about where you will spend eternity, which is so much longer than one lifetime.

The signing of a peace treaty between Israel and its Muslim neighbors marks the countdown of the seven years of the tribulation. This will happen, since the previous predictions of Daniel were found to be extremely accurate. Archaeologists have found sufficient, credible evidence to state with confidence that the Book of Daniel was written about 2,600 years ago. Legend has it that Alexander the Great was shown the part of the prediction that applied to him. He was so impressed that he ordered a Greek translation of the Old Testament—the Septuagint—so named because it was rushed through by seventy scholars. Others have one of Alexander's generals, Ptolemy or Ptolemy II, ordering the Septuagint. Regardless, there are extant copies of this manuscript housed in London and Rome, and they were written before the time of Christ. Alexander died in 323 BC.

In addition to the Book of Daniel, Revelation—the last book of the Bible—is a major source of information concerning the end times, including the tribulation. There are many New Testament manuscripts, some of them dated quite close to the original writing. These documents confirm by their consistency that this was the vision recorded by the Apostle John while under the influence of the Holy Spirit.

THE SEALS

During the first half of the tribulation, the wrath of God will begin with the four seals judgments known as the four horsemen of the apocalypse. This spiritual metaphor was given to John in Revelation to explain what would happen on Earth over 1,900 years later. The four horses represent various major calamities. The white horse represents a person—the antichrist. The red horse represents war. The black horse stands for worldwide drought, famine, disease, and inflation. The pale horse stands for death. The time is the first half of the tribulation. The following are the harrowing details of the beginning of the seven-year tribulation.

The first seal, judgment, involves a rider on a white horse, wearing a crown, with a bow but no arrows (Revelation 6:1–2). This is the politically strong antichrist, who uses diplomacy and deceit to bring a false peace to the Middle East. All will then know definitely who the antichrist is, for he will be the one who designs and brokers the peace between Israel and the surrounding Muslim nations.

Many worthy Bible scholars dispute this analysis and say that the man on the white horse is Jesus. But this does not make sense on several levels. First, Jesus does not arrive with a bow and no arrows, but with a sword. Second, the timing is off; Jesus rides in at the very end of the tribulation. Finally, it is logical that the antichrist, not Jesus, precedes the destructive horses that follow.

Daniel 8:23 indicates that the antichrist will assume worldwide power during the seven seal judgments. Apparently, he will set up a regional power structure with the strongest nations of the world heading up each of ten regions. The kings of these nations are the "ten horns" referenced in Revelation 13:1. Three of these nations will realize belatedly that they have given absolute power to a madman and try to do something about it—perhaps threaten the antichrist militarily. Daniel 7:24 says that these nations will be subdued, and there will be a very high death toll according to Revelation 6:8.

THE SECOND SEAL

The second seal judgment is that scenario played out. It is depicted as a rider on a red horse, which represents war—in this case, World War III (Revelation 6:3–4). The three kings that oppose the antichrist will challenge him militarily, and this will rapidly degenerate into a nuclear holocaust (Daniel 7:23–24). Over a billion people will eventually die in this war, which may include other weapons of mass destruction such as chemical or biological agents. The three nations will be crushed by the antichrist.

To complete this reasoned scenario and to carry prophecy to a logical conclusion, it is possible that the three nations are the United States, Brazil, and Japan, and that they will be largely destroyed without warning by a preemptive nuclear strike ordered by the antichrist. The first wave of bombings will literally wipe out the urban populations of these countries, which rules out an effective counter-strike. One fourth of the world's population will be destroyed without a backward glance from this man of evil (Revelation 6:8).

Why these three nations? The United States would be the logical head of the North American region; Brazil, the largest economy in South America, would be picked to head up that region. Japan, currently the second-largest economy in the world after the U.S., would be an appropriate selection to head up South Asia. The three nations have obvious ties and common interests that would lead one to expect that they would act together.

Brazil and the U.S. represent the Western Hemisphere, and Brazil's recent oil discoveries will also tie the two nations together. Japan and the U.S. will still have mutual defense interests, as they do today. This prediction alone should send chills into every American who is too proud. The Bible does seem to say that the United States is not quite as important to world stability as Americans always thought. The Middle East is the stage for Armageddon, and the U.S. does not even get a mention.

Many have asked what happens to the U.S. during end times because, as a nation, it seems to be strangely absent from these events. The U.S. has always enjoyed a privileged position with God, but that is largely because they have always defended and come to the aid of Israel, but already we can see that resolve that once existed weakening. So that privileged status will no longer be the case after the rapture. America's protection as a Christian nation and Israeli ally is removed, which frees its enemies to attack it. Also, there is no evidence in scripture to indicate that any Western Hemisphere nations take part in the battle of Armageddon, the last battle in Revelation.

THE NEXT THREE

The third seal judgment, represented by a rider on a black horse, reveals worldwide drought, famine, disease, and rampant inflation (Revelation 6:5–6). These are all things that could be expected after a nuclear war, as food untouched by radiation will be in very short supply. Weather patterns will be altered, and disease should flourish in an environment in which most sanitary and health care facilities have been destroyed. The survivors may well come to envy the dead.

The fourth seal judgment is depicted as a rider on a pale horse, which means death (Revelation 6:7–8). Shortly into the tribulation—about twenty-one months, or one-quarter of the seven years—twenty-five percent of the humans on Earth will have died. This would amount to about 1.5 billion persons if today's population were to be maintained. These people will die from war, starvation, and wild animals. Apparently wild animals, deprived of their natural environments and prey, will find the sick and injured humans an easy source of food. The first four seals reflect judgments that come about by the activities of man.

The fifth seal is broken, and it shows the Christian martyrs calling out from heaven for justice (Revelation 6:9–11). Some of these are tribulation saints, converted by the 144,000 witnesses but killed by the antichrist. The 144,000 witnesses are converted Jews—12,000 from each of the twelve tribes of Israel—who are successful in converting some of the unsaved on Earth after the rapture and during the tribulation (Revelation 7:3–8). These new Christians will be forced to make an immediate decision: Take the mark of the beast (the antichrist) or die. The martyrs are calling on God to stop this horrible process.

The sixth seal judgment is a supernatural judgment by God. The Apostle John describes an earthquake so large that every "mountain and island was moved out of its place" (Revelation 6:12–17). In addition, what appear to be asteroids strike the earth, causing great damage.

The seventh seal, which is the last of the seven seal judgments, introduces the seven trumpet judgments. The opening of the seventh seal results in an ominous silence in heaven for one half of an hour (Revelation 8:1–2). The trumpet judgments will be even worse than the seal judgments, and they are only about one-quarter through the tribulation. The wrath of God will now be felt during the second quarter of the tribulation, or the next twenty-one months.

THE TRUMPETS

The first trumpet will result in ice, fire, and blood raining down from the sky and burning up a third of the trees on Earth and all of the grass (Revelation 8:7). Some have speculated that this would be the natural fallout from a general nuclear attack, but no one knows for sure because there has never been a widespread nuclear war.

The second trumpet blows, and the Apostle John sees something that appears like a great, burning mountain crashing into the sea (Revelation 8:8–9). This may be another huge asteroid. Nevertheless, the results are catastrophic, as one-third of everything living in the sea and one-third of the ships on the sea are destroyed. The affected seawater will turn to blood.

The third trumpet sounds, and another asteroid crashes to Earth (Revelation 8:10–11). This falls on one-third of the earth's rivers and streams, turning them bitter and poisonous. As a result, many more will be killed.

The fourth trumpet sounds, and somehow, a third of the sun is darkened as well as one-third of all the heavenly bodies (Revelation 8:12). Luke tells us that people will die of fear at this time (Luke 21:25–26).

The fifth trumpet judgment releases thick, dark, smoke from the bottomless pit, and out of the smoke comes something like locusts. These locusts can sting man, but the sting will not kill them—only torture them with unbearable pain for five months (Revelation 9:1–11). The locusts will only attack those who do not have the seal of God on their foreheads. Thus, the saved will escape this particular torment.

The sixth trumpet blows and releases four angels, who proceed to lead an army of 200 million horsemen who then kill a third of mankind (Revelation 9:13–19). At about the halfway point of the tribulation, one-half of the world's population will have been destroyed. At today's level, this would represent three billion persons, and the battle of Armageddon has yet to take place.

The seventh trumpet blows, and all heaven is depicted rejoicing in what will soon be the victory of Christ over the antichrist. Meanwhile, on Earth, lightning, noise, hail, and another earthquake terrorize those who have survived (Revelation 11:15–19).

SUMMATION

To sum up the first half of the tribulation, one-half of the world's population will be killed in a number of nightmarish ways. During this period, warring armies continue to create death and havoc around the globe.

We need to read these warnings and take them very seriously while there is still time and there are still choices to make. These perilous times are the ones that are leading directly to the tribulation. These are no ordinary circumstances that the Bible speaks of: hail, fire, the waters turning to blood, and being stung by giant insects and suffering immeasurable pain for five months. Perhaps worst of all is dying because the fear of what may happen next is so great.

We know what Christ went through in the Garden of Gethsemane. His anguish was manifested as He sweated clots of blood because He knew what lay ahead for Him. Imagine something of that magnitude happening to mere humans. Fear brings torment, and torment is like hell on earth. Perhaps at that point death is a welcomed relief. However, hard as it may seem to believe, things proceed to get worse in the second half of the tribulation.

TAKING THE MARK

Those who are still alive at the halfway point of the tribulation, all of remaining mankind, will be faced with a daunting choice: Will they take the mark of the beast and ensure survival for a little while, or will they refuse to take it and be killed by the beast? That choice will be most unpleasant—take the mark or die.

If accepted they will be exposed to the full wrath of God on Earth, as well as spending all eternity in hell. However, it will not seem like such a clear-cut decision at that time. People will be much more conditioned to accept this mark. It will be viewed like credit cards were in the sixties—an easy way to get what you wanted or needed *now* without paying until later and it eliminates the worry of theft or loss of any kind. Getting a chip implanted one time will make life even simpler. It will enable you to do the same things only without the bother of having to carry a credit card or money.

What is the mark of the beast? In the past, much has been made about how such a thing could happen, and now, thanks to technology it is no longer science fiction. In fact it's easy to imagine something planted subcutaneously to identify the population of the world. Microchips are everywhere.

IT'S BEGUN

They are already used for identification purposes in animals. Today, people are ready to embed tiny computer chips into children so that they can be located if they are kidnapped. This seems like a laudable goal, but the door will then swing wide open, setting the stage for this wonderful technological breakthrough that will discourage if not eliminate purse snatchers and pickpockets, as well as many break-ins. It sounds too good to be true.

Everyone who takes this simple implant under their skin will no longer have to carry money or even credit cards. That little number will identify you and act as a debit card to your accounts. The problem is that once you take that implant, it brands you as belonging to Satan.

The numbers 666 must be included sequentially in the mark of the beast (Revelation 13:18). If you refuse to take it, you will not be able to conduct any business—to buy or sell anything; if you do take the mark, you will incur the wrath of God (Revelation 14:9–11).

WAY BACK IN THE EIGHTIES

Back in the eighties, when asked to write on the subject of a cashless society, it seemed farfetched. Now, after the end of the first decade in the twenty-first century—really only a few years later—the question is, "What can we do to slow this movement down?" With the advent of the home computer, online banking, ATMs, debit and credit cards, bar codes, PayPal on the Internet, and smaller and smaller computer chips, the technology is all in place for the cashless society; better than a one-world currency.

There are some major advantages to a cashless society. First, crime will take a dramatic downturn without cash. Second, it will be much more difficult to evade paying your fair share of taxes. The IRS believes that the underground economy reduces at least ten percent of the total taxes collected each year from taxes collected. So this cashless society could seem to be a very good thing; not only would it be more convenient, but it would reduce crime and enhance tax collection, perhaps even resulting in reduced taxes. It would also allow all to move freely from one place on Earth to another. You could travel around the world with no currency exchange or fear of robbery or loss.

We have reached the time in history where several things have happened to make this transference easy and practical. It began with credit cards, which made it easy to not have to carry cash. In many business establishments, large denomination bills aren't even accepted today. The possibility of One-World Government is close enough to be a reality. The UN is certainly there in its thinking, and the EU has fallen right in step with them. This could be quite convenient to live with—this cashless society. No more credit cards to deal with; just read the person's forehead or hand.

DRAWBACKS?

Of course, with such an implant, government employees will have access to your files and will literally be able to control each individual's life. Computer-savvy criminals and dishonest employees will have a certain amount of success in doing the same thing. At no time in the history of man will your rights as an individual be in such a precarious position. We have already discovered one unfortunate side effect of the cashless society—identity theft. About all a clever crook needs is one piece of information—a Social Security number, a bank or credit account number, or the like. In short order, that person can build up a complete file on you, including your financial and medical records, and use it themselves or sell it to others. Your personal financial and credit records can be destroyed or tainted for years.

It seems we have not learned much from our experiences with our Social Security cards; that little bit of paper that was originally distributed so that we could collect our retirement money. The number, our government guaranteed, would not become a national ID number, but guess what? It is exactly that. One cannot open a bank account or pay a phone bill, or even get information, without giving that number, which personally identifies him.

Still, like sheep being led to the slaughter, we give up our personal, national ID number to anyone who asks. We so readily use that number that we have to be reminded not to do this to strangers over the telephone or on the Internet. We have been conditioned to accept this practice, in the name of convenience, security, etc., but we should not be surprised when it all backfires on us. No matter how many privacy laws are passed, it only takes a few unscrupulous individuals to work around them.

IT'S ALREADY HERE

Getting people to accept the implantation of a chip should be a snap. We already have it in our pets. What a wonderful thing! If our precious animals go astray, they can be tracked by the simple implantation of a chip when they are very young. It has worked well over the past few years in reuniting lost pets and their owners.

Now we find that one in three hospitals and birthing centers are using a digital protection system for infant protection. The major company providing this modern marvel is called VeriChip and is based in Florida. (VeriChip Corp.com 2006, 1). VeriChip Corporation and Alzheimer's Community Care launched a patient identification project in 2007. Its application for these patients is probably very necessary. The problem is where will it end up?

VeriChip develops, markets, and sells radio frequency identification, or RFID, systems used to identify, locate, and protect people and assets. They are the forerunners in this new industry. VeriChip is now marketing the VeriMed Patient Identification System "for rapidly and accurately identifying people who arrive in the emergency room and are unable to communicate" (Veri-Medinfo.com 2007, 1).

We are witnesses to history being made and prophecy being fulfilled, all at the same time! The aforementioned system "uses the first human-implantable passive RFID chip cleared for medical use in October 2004 by the U.S. Food and Drug Administration."

NOW WE CAN BE BRANDED

There's more good news for proponents of this great new technology, which allows us all to eventually be branded like cattle and tracked in any or all of our everyday dealings. Once you agree to this miracle of science, there will be no more concern about being robbed—neither the individual nor places of business. No need to keep track of something tangible like money, credit cards, etc. Women may not even have to carry a purse! There will be no need for several forms of identification. Everything will be neatly wrapped up in one package—children, pets, money, and ID—all for our protection. Who could ask for more?

This is slowly being introduced and will continue to seep into our society and will be touted as the invention of the age. No one will see a downside. The whole idea of an antichrist and a beast will be laughed at, and thus, another seemingly impossible prophecy will be fulfilled.

Just remember the devil has worked long and hard to make himself this unbelievable. The Bible warned us of this day thousands of years ago, and every preceding generation has scoffed at even its possibility. Today the likelihood is right in front of us, yet still there are many scoffers touting the virtues of human implantation. It's a choice we'll all have to make, and it will be very costly to say no.

Be forewarned—the Bible puts it this way: "He causes all, both small and great, rich and poor, free and slave, to receive a mark on their right hand or on their foreheads, and that no one may buy or sell except one who has the mark of or the name of the beast, or the number of his name. Here is wisdom. Let him who has understanding calculate the number of the beast, for it is the number of a man: His number is 666" (Revelation 13:16–18).

It is apparent the way that this mark will go. Things will not be as rosy as those in charge will try to tell us, and let us not forget the biggest drawback of all. Once the antichrist is able to talk us into a one world, cashless monetary system, he will control our lives. Actually, he will control the entire world. There will be no more choices to make; they will all be made for us. He will be the puppeteer and we his marionettes! Keep that in mind as that day approaches.

A "BEASTLY" ASSASSINATION

Just prior to the midpoint of the tribulation, an amazing thing will happen. The antichrist will be killed, apparently by a wound—possibly gunshot—to the head. As billions of people watch his funeral on worldwide TV, it will then appear that he has been raised from the dead by the false prophet (Revelation 13:11–14). The whole world will marvel and follow the beast (Revelation 13:3). This seeming miracle will cement his claim to godhood. This event will cause many to follow the antichrist.

The antichrist will then make a decision that really brings down the wrath of God; he decides that it is time to break the treaty with Israel and cause his own image to be erected in the temple the Israelis have built in Jerusalem (Daniel 9:27).

Satan will indwell the antichrist at this point and finally achieve what he wanted since he rebelled in heaven eons ago. By his temptation of Jesus in the desert it is obvious that his heart's desire is to be worshiped like God. In fact, he will insist that all bow down and worship him or be executed (Revelation 13:15). His timing is impeccable, since most of the people of the world will be convinced he is God and are prepared to worship the reincarnated antichrist. Satan will then occupy the body of the antichrist for the remainder of the tribulation. Note that, according to Revelation 17:8, when the antichrist is slain at the midpoint of the tribulation, he descends into Hades and then is resurrected to Earth. Thus, the antichrist imitates the death and resurrection of Christ.

A NEW BABYLON

During this time, the antichrist will set up a commercial capital in a place the Bible refers to as Babylon. This could be a rebuilt Babylon or one of a number of pre-existing world cities that might strike the antichrist's fancy. One might assume that this would be a European city, as it would be most familiar to the antichrist. However, the Bible is not clear about which city this may be. Many have speculated that it might be Rome, as there is an end-times scripture relating to seven hills, and Rome was the capital city of the original Roman Empire.

In any event, this city will become a true world city; the important members of the global community will house their headquarters there. The antichrist plans to have total control over the world's economy, and he will accomplish that during the second half of the tribulation. By then, everyone will be given the mark of the beast—666 (Revelation 13:18). All those without the mark will be killed by the antichrist.

That choice would involve rejecting the message of Christ as delivered by the 144,000 witnesses and others during the tribulation. This scenario is no more pleasing to God than the temple worship of the antichrist. Thus, it can be said without exaggeration that the full wrath of God will be poured out during the second half of the tribulation.

Once again, for those who think that this is an exaggeration; remember that the Bible has an extremely high accuracy rate for fulfilled prophecy—for events predicted that have already come to pass. There is no reason to believe that the tribulation predictions will vary from this.

THE LAST 42 MONTHS

The second half of the tribulation begins with the bowl judgments being carried out. These are God's judgments on man and are primarily directed at the wicked and unsaved. The first bowl judgment involves the infliction of boils on those who accept the mark of the beast and worship him. These boils are described as grievous in Revelation 16:2.

In the second bowl judgment, the sea becomes as the blood of a dead man, as recorded in Revelation 16:3. As a result, every creature in the ocean dies. If you have ever seen or smelled a dead fish, you have some idea how horrible the sight and stench will be. It would appear that such a massive death would make the coastlines of all nations uninhabitable and an ideal breeding ground for disease.

The third angel pours out his bowl on the rivers and springs and "they became blood" (Revelation 16:4). This would indicate that every source of Earth's fresh water will have been contaminated—a just punishment for those who have shed the blood of the saints. They have now been given "blood to drink" (Revelation 16:6).

The fourth angel pours out his bowl on the sun, and "men were scorched with great heat" (Revelation 16:9). Strangely enough, rather than repent, they "...blasphemed the name of God..." You would think that everyone who is left on Earth would repent of their evil deeds and fall down and worship the true God of the universe. Their hearts are truly hardened, and this is not to be the case.

THE FIFTH BOWL

Then, the fifth angel will pour out his bowl "...on the throne of the beast, and his kingdom became full of darkness; and they gnawed their tongues because of the pain." Yet they still blaspheme and do not repent (Revelation 16:10–11).

The angel then poured the sixth bowl out on the Euphrates River, "...and its water was dried up..." Three unclean spirits emerge from the mouths of the unholy counterfeit trinity and go to the kings of the earth to encourage them to bring armies to Armageddon for the final battle (Revelation 16:12–14).

The last angel pours his bowl into the air, and a loud voice from heaven says, "…It is done!" (Revelation 16:17). A great earthquake destroys commercial Babylon, and all the great cities fall. Giant hailstones fall on man, yet they continue to blaspheme God.

This concludes the bowl judgments and what remains is the battle of Armageddon, the second coming, and the millennium. By this point, all of the judgments have been completed, with the exception of the Great White Throne Judgment, which takes place after the millennium; the world and its population have been decimated. Now you would assume that most people would have had enough of the wars and supernatural disasters and would be willing to do just about anything to keep the peace, but that is not so.

ARMAGEDDON

These demons (bowl six) are masters of deceit. They perform miraculous signs and thereby convince the leaders to assemble their armies, where there will be one final battle. Some experts feel that there will be up to four battles in this campaign, but the purpose remains the same. This great army is assembled to fight against Judah and Jerusalem. The demons and their armies are battling the Israelis when Jesus suddenly appears and they find themselves warring against the Son of God.

The Apostle John records what he saw concerning this battle.

> And I saw the beast, the kings of the earth, and their armies, gathered together to make war against Him that sat on the horse (Jesus) and against his army. Then the beast was captured, and with him the false prophet who worked signs in his presence, by which he deceived those who received the mark

of the beast and those who worshiped his image. The two were cast alive into the lake of fire burning with brimstone. And the rest were killed with the sword which proceeded from the mouth of Him who sat on the horse. And all the birds were filled with their flesh.

(Revelation 19:19–21)

Some may find it foolish that human armies would dare to take on a supernatural foe. The folly of human beings coming against the Creator of the universe is immeasurable. However, in their defense, they had no advance idea that they would be battling Jesus. They were also under the very crafty deception of the demons sent to recruit them. The kings, believing the lying spirits, thought they would be fighting those defending Israel and naturally expected them to be mortal men. The results, of course, are very predictable. Everyone will be destroyed except for the antichrist and the false prophet, who will be thrown alive into a burning lake of fire. Satan is bound in a pit.

THEY CHOSE SIDES

Many critics of Christianity ask how God could be ruthless toward people and yet claim to be a God of love. God is a God of love, but his patience does not extend for all time. Those killed in the battle of Armageddon had chance after chance to repent, and they did not. They were willing to attack Jesus and foolish enough to think they could somehow win. These are evil people who will have chosen sides knowingly; they have little conscience and no compunction about killing innocents.

Many of those men killed in the battle of Armageddon will be leaders. They will be intelligent men who had the opportunity of salvation offered by the 144,000 Jewish witnesses during the tribulation. In fact, there will be a great soul harvest, and those who are left are truly the incorrigible and wicked with "seared consciences." The Bible states that some people will become so used to sinning that they have their consciences hardened to the point where the Holy Spirit can no longer be heard. In this case, they will be self-centered, greedy individuals who will believe the promises coming from lying spirits.

Always remember that God created us with one wonderful gift that separates from the rest of creation; that gift is free will. God could have made us puppets and made all the decisions for us, but He wanted us to choose to know Him and to choose to love Him. Everyone has many chances to make the choice for themselves. Those that do perish will have exercised their free will. They choose to go against goodness, but God is loving and is merciful, even to the most evil of men, when they repent.

A DIFFERENT JESUS

Have you noticed that the man on the white charger at the battle of Armageddon doesn't much resemble the humble man beaten and spit upon by Roman soldiers? That's because He is not the same man—at least not in design. When Jesus came to us the first time, He was born in a stable and grew up to be a meek man, enduring mockery, rejection, and crucifixion. He was the consummate suffering servant. He became poor so that we might become rich. He came with reconciliation in mind—to bear the sins and diseases of the world, to provide redemption, and to give us a way to be restored to God the Father. His death and resurrection accomplished all of this.

When Jesus returns, He will appear in His full might, power, and majesty. He will ride from the clouds on a white horse. This is more the image that the Jews have always had of their Messiah. The sword in His mouth is the spoken word. He merely spoke, and He brought the universe and all its inhabitants into existence (Genesis 1). He will speak then, and the armies at Armageddon will be destroyed. Jesus will have a totally different objective for His second coming—to defeat all the forces of evil and establish God's kingdom on Earth.

THE NEW MILLENNIUM AND BEYOND

The tribulation ends with the battle of Armageddon, and the Millennium follows. Satan is bound in a bottomless pit for a period of a thousand years, and everyone lives in a perfect world. Life is long and worry and sickness free, in a place too beautiful for human description. People will experience the wonder and beauty that Adam and Eve lost after the fall. Then, after the thousand years, Satan is loosed from the pit. Those who have never been tested or tempted during the millennium will now have a choice to make, a side to choose. Immediately, even after a thousand years of bliss, Satan is able to raise large armies of those who would go against God.

"They went up on the breadth of the earth and surrounded the camp of the saints and the beloved city. And fire came down from God out of heaven and devoured them. The devil, who deceived them, was cast into the lake of fire and brimstone where the beast and false prophet are. And they will be tormented day and night forever and ever" (Revelation 20:9–10).

Once again, we see man's sinful nature rise up. Man is inherently evil. Jeremiah 17:9 tells us, "The heart is deceitful above all things, and desperately wicked..." The proof of that is the Millennium itself. Men live in absolute peace and perfection for a thousand years, and then they rise against the one providing it; they are either saturated with evil or just plain stupid.

The Bible is quite specific that, through deception, Satan will have no problem raising a huge army to fight God "...to gather them together to battle, whose number is as the sand of the sea" (Revelation 20:8).

A NEW HEAVEN AND EARTH

After the Millennium, there will be a new heaven and a new earth, which are discussed by the Apostle John in Revelation 21. In this paradise, there will be no more tears and no more death, sorrow, or pain. He goes on to describe the "...holy city, New Jerusalem, coming down out of heaven from God..."

The length, breadth, and height of this new city will be equal; it will be a cube that will be suspended in mid-air. It will be surrounded by a great wall made of jasper, and the foundation will be garnished with precious stones. There will be twelve gates made of pearl, each made from one pearl, "...And the street of the city was pure gold, like transparent glass." There will be no sun or moon and no artificial light there because it will never get dark; God's presence will illuminate it. There will be no need for a temple to worship in because God and Jesus are the temples.

John continues in Revelation 22 with his description, saying there will be "...a pure river of water of life, clear as crystal, proceeding from the throne of God and of the Lamb." This river will be the water supply for the whole earth, since there will be no sea (Revelation 21:1). It will support all of the vegetation needed for the entire world. Imagine that! The universal water supply will emanate from the throne of God.

In the middle of the street, on either side of the river, there is the tree of life, which yields twelve different fruits every month. "The leaves of the tree were for the healing of the nations" (Revelation 22:2).

THERE IS A CHOICE

In this infinite universe, with an eternity of time, we will have plenty to do. We will have enjoyable, satisfying, and fruitful work. There will be meaning and gladness to our lives and plenty of spare time to indulge in other pleasures.

This entire description has been taken from the Bible. It's hard to fathom such a place and such a time, but we have God's Word on it. For the many who have gone before us, their decision time is over, but you and I can still make the right choice and choose God and all the wonders that come with Him.

It has become unfashionable to discuss hell, but it is a real place and not some spiritualized, no-rules place where you will hang out with your old drinking buddies and swap war stories. Hell will be very unpleasant and very permanent.

Matthew 13:42 says, "And will cast them into the furnace of fire. There will be wailing and gnashing of teeth." Torment, torture, and misery for eternity doesn't sound like a good thing, but in case you still are not certain, here is a more official definition of the place called hell.

Smith's Bible Dictionary tells us that in the New Testament, the word *Gehenna* is used twelve times for the place of future, eternal punishment. "This was originally the valley of Hinnom, south of Jerusalem, where the filth and dead animals of the city were cast out and burned—a fit symbol of the wicked and their destruction." It had become the common cesspool of the city, into which sewage flowed, to be carried off by the Kidron. The word Hinnom (Gehenna) means "the place of eternal torment." Jesus speaks of this garbage dump, with which all of the Jews are familiar, to explain what those who elect not to follow Him can expect.

There are many more descriptions of hell in the Bible; it is a pit of darkness without any light at all. There are no distractions from the agony, fears, sorrow, and suffering. It is a place of physical agony, mental suffering, and extreme loneliness. It is a place of uncertainty—a bottomless pit where every minute is lived in fear. It is a permanent separation from God and all things good—a place of destruction, of constant pain, and insecurity (Revelation 20).

FROM THOSE WHO'VE BEEN THERE

Hell is described and spoken of over and over in the Bible, often by Jesus. Words seem to be limited when it comes to defining the horrendous, yet you need to know and understand that it is a real place. We all need to know it, and telling you from a strictly biblical standpoint seems to promote skepticism. However, when you hear the words of real people—medical personnel who have witnessed these events and hospital patients who have experienced firsthand the horror and hopelessness of an eternity in the bowels of the earth—it makes a difference.

With the advent of new medical procedures, it is now possible to bring people back to life who have been clinically dead for some period of time. In fact, this happens quite frequently in the emergency room and at the scene of automobile and other accidents. According to Dr. Maurice S. Rawlings, a cardiologist and expert researcher in near-death experiences (NDE), eleven million Americans have experienced NDEs or out-of-body experiences.

Initially, many medical experts ascribed the stories that NDE survivors told as being the result of oxygen-deprived brains. However, as more data was accumulated, it became clear that this was not the answer. Some of the survivors told their stories from a physical viewpoint above their body and added details that they could not have known or seen lying on an operating table or on the ground at an automobile wreck site. Also, many people with NDEs found their experiences to be vivid and life-altering, often telling similar stories when compared to others who experienced the same.

While many NDE survivors told of peaceful, loving trips to heaven—having a life review with God, as well as discussions with dead friends and relatives—not all fell in this category. Some came back to life claiming vivid recollections of being in hell. The following description of Hell is not from a religious book, the man who wrote it is a cardiologist. The book contains true life experiences of his patients resuscitated back to life. The following is one of his patients telling of their experience.

> I was guided to a place in the spirit world called Hell. This is a place of punishment for all those who reject Jesus Christ. I not only saw Hell, but felt the torment that all who go there experience. The darkness of Hell is so intense that it seems to have a pressure per square inch. It is an extremely black, dismal, desolate, pressurized, heavy type of darkness. It gives the individual a despondent feeling of loneliness. The heat is a dry,

dehydrating type; your eyeballs are so dry they feel like red-hot coals in their sockets. Your tongue and lips are parched and cracked with intense heat—The loneliness of Hell cannot be expressed.

(Rawlings 2010, 75)

MORE NDE'S

Bill Weise, who wrote 23 *Minutes in Hell,* wrote that he saw "searing flames of hell, felt total isolation, and experienced the putrid and rotting stench, deafening screams of agony, terrorizing demons."

(Weise 2006)

Others have interviewed large numbers of people who had negative Near Death Experiences, and they all have one message: There is a hell, and you don't want to end up there. In short, if you don't believe what your Bible has to say on this subject, take it from us. Hell is a real place, and you don't want anything to do with it.

By the way, some of these NDE researchers are successful non-theologians who do not need to write books on this subject to augment their income or improve their standing as Christian celebrities. For instance, Dr. Rawlings is a physician to the Joint Chiefs of Staff, Associate Clinical Professor of Medicine at the University of Tennessee, and a diplomat of the American Board of Cardiology, among other achievements.

Like many other medical personnel and ER physicians, Dr. Rawlings is struck by the fact that seriously injured but conscious people of all faiths seem to have one comment when they appear on the operating table—"God, help me!" It seems that they just can't keep from saying this.

When in excruciating pain that cancer drugs cannot relieve, the patient always calls out to God. The words are always the same: "God, help me!" He will help you, but you must make that decision while you are alive; it must be made from a position of faith. You must believe it before you see it. The good news is that anyone reading this book has a choice—the opportunity to decide for himself: heaven or hell.

THE TIME IS NOW

There have been many novels written that do not have the excitement and drama that real life is about to unfold. Even the wonderful stories about the end times, with all their special effects on huge screens, cannot hope to capture what God has in store over the next few decades. If you don't think this time is ultra exciting, the problem is your vantage point. Most Christians are thrilled with the idea of these last days. The only downside for them is the millions of lives that will choose not to be on the right side and will perish. For those it will truly be a time of devastation.

The world is getting smaller every day, while egos are getting bigger. If the power elite have their way, it will soon be joined together under one government, one monetary system, and one religion. So what happens to one will happen to all. There will be no safe place, no haven of peace or neutrality. And what the power-hungry elite have not considered is if a leader, a treacherous, unconscionable dictator, takes over. The signs are there, but many are not aware of them: the tsunami that killed hundreds of thousands, the earthquakes and hurricanes that have hit all over the world in record numbers. Nuclear weapons and other WMD's are in the hands of madmen who could blow up half the world with the push of a button.

And closer to home, a society that has turned its back on God and its forefathers. A self-centered, materialistic, atheistic America has emerged from the decades of instant gratification that we all went through, where it seemed easy to have it all with little payback. Now we are a nation divided right down the middle in ideology, politics, morals, and future...because the future of many is as bleak as the rest of the world.

We who have lived through a calamity like a tornado or an earthquake may think we've seen our darkest day. Those who have survived cancer or a stroke or heart attack believe that it's all good from here. The many who have suffered financial ruin in a bad economy and have lost everything they worked so hard for feel they have endured the worst that life can dish out. But even the betrayal of a dear friend or the loss of a loved one cannot compare with the days to come.

Those caught in the tribulation will see and experience horrors that the mind cannot conceive. We'd like to think that Revelation is just a book of symbolism and Armageddon is just another war, but the truth is they are just what they say they are. Deceit at its greatest, devastation at its worst, and destruction at its most complete. Pain and agony and loss and sorrow beyond measure. We cannot imagine, not can it be put to paper what lies ahead...directly ahead. We are all on a collision course with destiny.

TAKE THE OPPORTUNITY

The world has been fooled into waiting for a special invitation. They are deceived into thinking that there will be plenty of time and that they will see anything negative coming, but the fact is they won't! Too many, unfortunately, will make no choice, and that could prove deadly, for the decision will be made for them. You see, God is a gentleman, and He waits for people to come to Him, unlike His adversary Satan, who will gladly and cunningly confuse and entrap you.

Before continuing, it may be that all the terrible things you've done in your life have suddenly come to your attention. That does not matter. We are all sinners, and yet God loves all of us. The size of the sin is of no consequence. King David committed both adultery and murder, yet God called him "a man after my own heart." If you feel that your list of sins and transgressions is too long to count, then remember Marcia's story; she is alive and well today and was once totally immersed in the occult. Nothing could blaspheme the Lord God more than someone who chooses to become close friends with evil, and she was in the depths of it.

In Marcia's own words, "Spiritually, I had been in a grave with the Buddhas and the sorcerers and the seekers of wisdom who had rejected the truth of Christ. The complicated and intricate studies that enthralled me, the endless layers of truth and realities I had pursued, the constant effort to evolve, the paranormal experiences, the need to believe in one's own goodness at all costs, were all a maze and a trap. The truth was simple enough for a child because the truth is a person. Jesus did not teach the way or say He had a way. He said He is the way—not a way, but *the* way."

Marcia has turned to God and has learned the truth. Her life today is filled with purpose and direction, and her ministry CANA is a valuable resource for those in need. It answers your questions about the New Age from one who has been there, and it points to the way out for those who find themselves enmeshed in dark practices.

YOUR SPECIAL INVITATION

There is one major reason that this book has been written, the timing of which is somewhat different from the predictions of most experts. If God cared enough to impart to us nobodies some useful information, the purpose was to pass it on to you so that you can see how accurate the Bible is and how quickly things are really coming together. Now why would the Creator of the Universe care about you or this book? It's simple; it's because, as the Bible tells us, He loves us beyond belief and does not want one of us to perish (John 3:16, 2 Peter 3:9). Before getting to the climax of this real-life drama of the future, consider this your special invitation to choose to get on the right side.

Please know that God does not ask anything of you but to believe in Him and to accept, by faith, what Jesus has already done for you. It is a choice—your choice. If it is your heart's desire to be on the right side, to get to know God and His ways, and if you want to spend eternity in heaven, then there is only one thing you must do. Repeat the following sinner's prayer, or use your own words, and mean it in your heart.

Heavenly Father,

I come to you today choosing to be on your side. I believe that you loved me so much that you sent your only begotten Son, Jesus, to die for me, personally, on the cross. I also believe that He was resurrected from the dead. All of my past sins are forgiven, washed under His shed blood. I choose to make Jesus the Lord and Savior of my life and live for Him. I accept the free gift of eternal life that Christ already has provided for me. Amen.

FINALLY

Please say the special invitation prayer and choose eternal life. Now is the time for all to consider the not-too-distant future while there is still time to choose. God does not want to see one of His people perish, but He has given us free will. Here's what the Bible says about the coming decades:

> And, behold, I am coming quickly, and My reward is with Me, to give everyone according to his work.
>
> Revelation 22:12

There you have it—the entire future laid out for you. A Hitler-like despot called the antichrist will rise to power. He will eventually take over the EU and the UN and be a leader in the Trilateral Commision. Satan will be his source of power, and the false prophet will be his partner in crime. The New Age, or a version thereof, will be the religion of the world, and a promise of world peace will catapult the antichrist to being ruler of the earth. Lies and deceit will make a god of him until the one true God exacts his revenge. Everyone has a choice to make—a life-altering decision. It all seems simple and obvious enough, but it also seems obvious that people in paradise would not betray God at the end of the millennium; yet, they will by the millions.

> He who overcomes shall inherit all things, and I will be His God, and he shall be My son. But the cowardly, unbelieving, abominable, murderers, sexually immoral, sorcerers, idolaters, and all liars shall have their part in the lake which burns with fire and brimstone, which is the second death.
>
> Revelation 21:7–8

A second, continuous, never-ending death! If there is a spark within you that believes in God, heaven, and eternal life, then you must know that there is a flip side—the devil, hell, and eternal death, and darkness, loneliness, and pain. It is the permanent separation from all your loved ones and God Himself. Perhaps the saddest of all possible truths is that there never was and never will be one person in hell who does not believe in Jesus *now*.

BIBLIOGRAPHY

Abadi, Cameron, "Germany: How to fight neo-Nazis?," *Global Post*, February 12, 2010.

http://www.globalpost.com/dispatch/germany/100212/neo-Nazi-npd-party.

Adachi, Ken, "The New World Order (NWO): An Overview," *Educate-Yourself.org*, November 30, 2009, http://educate-yourself.org/nwo?.

Al-Tamimi, Aymenn Jawad, "The Muslim World Needs Reform," *Middle East Forum*, October 20, 2009, www.MEforum.org.

Anglebert, Jean-Michel, *The Occult and the Third Reich*, New York: McGraw Hill, 1975.

Aquarian Age Community Home Page, "About the Aquarian Age Community," *Aquarian age Community*, 2010, http://www.aquaac.org/about/about/html.

Arya, "The Nazi Secret Doctrine", *Strormfront. org.*, November 14, 2005, http://www.stormfront. org/forum/sitemap/index.php/t-246749.html.

Atlantic Monthly, "Mortal Fears," February, 1988, page 30, *Eagle Forum,* June 1999, http://www.eagleforum.org/psr/june99.html.

Atrayu, "Lucis Trust The Spiritual Foundation of the United Nations", *Freemasonry Watch, February* 13, 2007,http:// www.freemasonry watch.org/lucistrust.html.

Bailey, Alice A., *Discipleship in the New Age, Volume II,* New York: Lucis Trust Publishing, 1955.

Bailey, Alice A., *Education in the New Age,* New York: Lucis Trust Publishing, 1937.

Bailey, Alice A., *The Reappearance of the Christ,* New York: Lucis Publishing Company, 1948.

Bailey, Alice A., *The Externalization of the Hierarchy,* New York: Lucis Publishing Company, 1957.

Bailey, Alice A., *The Unfinished Autobiography,* New York: Lucis Trust Publishing, 1951.

Bauwens, Micheal, "Spirituality and Technology: Exploring The Relationship," *First Monday,* November 4, 1996, http://firstmonday.org/issues/issue5/bauwens/

BBC News, "Vatican Sounds New Age Alert," *BBC News World Edition,* February 4, 2003, http:// news.bbc.co.uk/2/hi/europe/2722743.stm.

Bedein, David, "Recalling the Man Who Inspired Hitler," *Israel National News.com,* April 15, 2007, http://www.israelnationalnews.com/Articles/Article.aspx/7056.

Bergman, Jerry, "Darwinism And The Nazi Race Holocaust," *Technical Journal,* November 1999, http://www.trueorigin.org/holocaust.asp.

Berkman, Gene, "The Trilateral Commission And The New World Order," *Copyright Gene Berkman,* January 1993, http://www.antiwar.com/berkman/trilat.html.

Bible Explained, "Islam in Bible Prophesy," *Bible Explained.com,* http://.bibleexplained.com/revelation/r-seg09–10/r09m-Islam.htm.

Biden, Joe, "How I learned to love the New World Order," *The Wall Street Journal,* April 23,1992, page A13.

Blavatsky, Helena, *The Secret Doctrine, Volumes 1 and 2,* Pasadena, CA: Theosophical University Press, 1888.

Bliss, Sylvester, *Memoirs of William Miller,* Boston: Joshua V. Himes, 1853.

Blue/Schwandorf, Laura "Lessons From Germany," *Time Magazine,* April 23, 2008.

Bonville, Bill, "What is Outcome Based Education (OBE)?," *Integraonline.com,* http://integraonline.com/~bonville//Education/WhatIsObe.html.

Brown, David L., "Adolph Hitler's Occult Connections," *Logos Resource Pages,* 1992, http://logos-resourcepages.org/hitler.html, 1992.

Brown, Robert M., "Division of Continual Learning Dean's Message," *The University of North Carolina, Greensboro,* October 12, 2009, http://web.uncg.edu/web/about/about_dean.asp.

Brownell, Eileen O., "Managing Change Successfully," *SOHO America,* 2000, http://www.soho.org/Start_Up_Articles/Managing_Change.htm.

Bush, George H. W., "—and the emerging New World Order we now see," *New York Times,* January 17, 1991, http://en.wikiquote.org/wiki/George_H._W._Bush.

Canisius Books, "New Age or Global Education: Terminology Used in New Age Education," *Canisius Books,* 2010, http://www.canisiusbooks.com/na_ed_chart.htm.

Cho David Yonggi, *The Apocalyptic Prophecy,* Orlando, FL: Creation House,1998.

Cirone, Marianne Woods, "Deliberate Creation and Yoga Philosophy," *Yoga, Health and Fitness,* 2010, http://www.yoga-for-health-and-fitness.com/deliberate-creation.html.

Cole, Julio H., "The Writings of Adam Smith," *The Freeman,* February 1990, http://thefreemasononline.org/columns/the-writings-of-adam-smith/.

Creme, Benjamin, "The Antahkarana," *Spiritual.com.au,* 2009, http://www.spiritual.com.au/articles/ascension/antahkarana-bcreme.htm.

Crèème, Benjamin, *The Awakening of Humanity,* London: Share International Foundation, 2008.

Crossland, David, "Neo-Nazi Threat Growing Despite NPD Cash Woes," *Spiegel Online International,* March 19, 2009, http://www.spiegal.de/international/germany/0,1518,614209.html.

Cumbey, Constance, *The Hidden Dangers of the Rainbow,* Lafayette, LA: Huntington House, Inc., 1983.

Daniel, Randolph E., "Medieval Apocalypticism: Looking for the Last Emperor," *Christianity Today Library.com,* January 1, 1999, http://www.christianitytoday.com/ch/1999/issue61/61h016.html.

Dick, Everett N., *William Miller and the Advent Crisis,* Berrien Springs, MI: Andrew University Press, 1994, page 27.

Dexter, Penna, "Oprah's New Age Gospel," *Baptist Press,* March 27, 2008, http://www.sbcbaptistpress.org/printerfriendly.asp?ID=27712.

Dirda, Michael, "Hitler's Private Library," *The Washington Post,* October 26, 2008, http://www.washingtonpost.com/wp-dyn/content/article/2008/10/23/AR2008102302662_p— (Review of William Ryback's book of the same name).

Dixon, Herti, "Anti-Semitism on The Rise in Europe," *Charisma Magazine,* May 2009, Lake Mary, FL: Strang Publishing Group, Page 26.

Dorsheimer, Craig, "Discovering the New Age Movement/New World Order, Part Three," *Truthspeaker,* September 5, 2008, http://truthspeaker.wordpress.com/2008/09/05/discovering-the-new-age-movement-new-—

Encarta Premium, "Holocaust," *Encarta Premium,* 2008, http://encarta.msn.com/text_761559508___0/Holocaust.html.

Europa, "A Brief History Of European Integration," *Europa.eu* ,2010, http://europa.eu.int/comm/publications/booklets/eu_glance/12/txt_en.htm.

Faith Christian Ministries, "How to Respond to The New Age Movement," *Faith Christian Ministries*, 2010, http://www.faithchristianmin.org/articles/newage.htm

Ferguson, Marilyn, *The Aquarian Conspiracy*, Los Angeles: J.P. Tarcher, 1980.

Frost, Ellen L., "From Rockets to Religion: Understanding Globalization," *European Union Studies Center*, October 6, 2000, http://web.gc.cuny.edu/Eusc/activies/paper/frost.ellen.htm.

Gavin, Phillip, "Genocide in the 20th Century," *The History Place*, November 6, 2000, http://www.historyplace.com/worldhistory/genocide/index.html.

Geocites.com, "Adolph Hitler is Born," *Geocites.com*, 2003, http://www.geocites.com/Athens/Rhodes/6146/index.html.

Geocities.com, "Germans Elect Nazis," *Geocities.com*, 2003, http://www.geocities.com/Athens/Rhodes/1188/page15.html.

Geocities.com, "Hitler Named Chancellor," *Geocities.com*, 2003, http://www.geocities.com/Athens/Rhodes/1188/page19.html.

Gospelcom.net, "Rise Of The Antichrist," *Gospelcom.net*, http://www.gospelcom.net/rbc/ds/q1201/point2.html.

Gordon, Cindy, "Wikis Are A Powerful Knowledge Accelerator," *Helixcommerce.com*, http://blogs.helixwikiconsulting.com/blog/2007/07/04/wikis-are-a-powerful-knowledge-acc ... ,

Gnostic Liberation Front, "Hitler, Nazis & the Occult," *Gnosticliberationfront.com*, January 3, 2010, www.grostictliberationfront.com/hitler,nazis%20and%20the%20occult.htm.

Graff, Ron, "Overview of Prophesy," *Overview of Prophesy*, August 9, 2008, http://www.bible-prophesy.com/overview.htm.

Grim, William E., "A Gentile's View of Today's Germany," *Christian Action For Israel*, February 2003, http://christianactionforisrael.org/antiholo/germany.html.

Grim, William, "Al Qaeda's Neo-Nazi Connections," *Jewish Post*, February 25, 2004, http://www.middleeast.org/forum/fb-public/1/4320.shtml.

Harding, Luke, "German neo-Nazis gain a platform by taking seats in a regional assembly," *Buzzle*.com, February 10, 2005, http://www.guardian.co.uk/world/2006/sep/18/germany.the farright.

Herald Tribune, "Raids target music promoting hatred," Stuttgart, Germany, *Sarasota Herald Tribune*, March 5, 2009, page 8A, www.herald tribune.com/world.

Hoeck, Kenneth M., "The History of Satan the Devil," *Stories, Jokes and* Poems, 2006, http://members.aol.com/KHoeck3?Gods.html.

Intelinet.org, "The Swastika and the Nazis," The Eckart Connection, *The Swastika and the Nazis*, 2008, http://www.intelinet.org/swastika/swastio8.htm

Internet Time.com, "Knowledge Management," *Internet Time Blog,* November 7, 2003, http://internettime.com/blog/archives/001081.html.

Israel Forum.com, "A Report On Nazism in the New Age Movement," *Israel Forum,* April 4, 2007, http://www.israelforum.com/board/showthread.php?t=12369

Janning, Josef, " Facts about Germany: Germany in Europe," *Facts about Germany,* April 16, 2010, http://www.tatsachen-ueber-deutschland.de.en/foreign-policy—

Jeremiah Project, "The New Age Agenda," *Jeremiah Project,* 2009,http://www.jeremiahproject.com/prophesy/newage02.html.

Jeremiah Project, "The New World Order," *Jeremiah Project,* 2009, http://www.jeremiahproject.com/prophesy/nworder.html.

Jones, Phillip, "Hitler And The New Age," *Rense.com,* June 28, 2009,rense.com/genera186/newagehit.htm

Joya, Alonso Soto, "Applied Digital Launches VeriChip Tracking in Mexico," *The Palm Beach Post,* July 19, 2003, Page 11B.

Kalish, Michael, "Frederich Nietzsche's Influence on Hitler's Mein Kampf," *Michael Kalish,* June 2004, http://www.history.ucsb,edu/faculty/mancuse/classes/1333p04papers/mkalish—

Kapner, Nathanael, "Neo-Nazi Rise In Germany Frightens Jews," *Real Zionist News,* 2009, http://www.realzionistnews.com/?p=390.

Kjos, Berit, "The Ominous "Success" of Re-education," *Crossroad to,* October 5, 2009, http://crossroad.to/articles2/009/3-family.htm.

Kuhner, Jeffrey T., "Obama's new world order," *The Washington Times* , October 25, 2009.

Kutilek, Douglas K., "Charles Darwin, Racist," *Sharperiron.org,* July 31, 2009, http://wwwhsharperiron.org/charles-darwin-racist.

LaHaye, Tim, *Revelation Unveiled,* Grand Rapids, MI: Zondervan Publishing House, 1999.

LaHaye, Tim and Jenkins, Jerry B., *Are We Living In The End Times?,* Wheaton, IL: Tyndale House Publishers, Inc., 1999.

LaFranchi, "A New World Order?," *Christian Science Monitor,* October 20, 2008, http://www.csmoniter.com/2001/0914/plsl-uspo.html.

Let Us Reason Ministries, "Hitler's Spiritual Master-Maitreya," *Let Us Reason Ministries,* 2009, www.letusreason.org/Nam%2037.htm.

Let Us Reason Ministries, "The Plan," *Let Us Reason Ministries,* 2009, http://letusreason.org/NAM20.htm.

Let Us Reason Ministries, "The Initiation", *Let Us Reason Ministries,* 2009, http://letusreason.org/NAM19.htm.

Let Us Reason Ministries, "The New Age Movement," *Let Us Reason Ministries,* 2009, http://www.letusreason.org/Nam4.htm.

Lindsay, Hal, *Apocalypse Code,* Palos Verdes, CA: Western Front, Ltd., 1997.

Lindsay, Hal, *Planet Earth-2000 A.D.*, Palos Verdes, CA: Western Front Ltd.,1994.

Lindsay, Hal, *The Late, Great Planet Earth,* Grand Rapids, MI: Zondervan Publishing, 1970.

Longgrear, Paul and McNemar, Raymond, "Anti-Semitism and Holocaust," *Christian Action For Israel,* 2003, http://www. Christianactionforisreal.org/recruited.html.

Looney, Michael, "The Need For Digital Archiving Standards", *Campus* Technology, October 20, 2004, http://campustechnology.com/articles/39100_1/.

Lynott, Douglas B., "Joseph Mengele," *Crime Library (TruTV),* 2010, http://www.crimelibrary.com/serial_killers/history/mengele/aus_4.html?sect=6.

Mapreport.com, "World Disasters, Famine Timeline, 21st Century," *Mapreprort.com,* April 14, 2010, http://www.mapreport.com/subtropics/do.html.

Martin, Malachi, *The Keys of This Blood,* New York: Touchstone, 1990

Maser, Werner, *Hitler: Legend, Myth and Reality,* New York: Random House, 1975.

McFee, Gord, "When Did Hitler Decide On The Final Solution?," *Gordon McFee,* January 2, 1999. http://www.holocaust-history.org/hitler-final-solution/.

Montenegro, Marcia, "Feng Shui: New Dimensions In Design," *Christian Answers For The New Age,* April 13, 2003, http://cana.userworld.com/cana_fengShui.html.

Montenegro, Marcia, "Marcia's Story: A Strange But True Spiritual Journey," *Christian Answers For The New Age,* 2008, http://www.christiananswersforthenew-age.org/AboutCANA_SpiritualJourney.html.

Montenegro, Marcia, "Yoga: Yokes, Snakes, And Gods," *Christian Answers For The New Age,* 2008, http://cana.userworld.com/cana_yoga.html.

Morse, Chuck, "The Nazi Connection to Islamic Terrorism—," *Amazon*.com, 2010, http://www.amazon.com/Nazi-Connection_Islamic_Terrorism-al-Hesseini/dp/0595289444.

Muller, Robert, *New Genesis: Shaping a Global Spirituality,* Garden City, NY: Doubleday/Image, 1984.

McDowell, Josh, *The New Evidence That Demands a Verdict,* Nashville: Thomas Nelson Publishers, 1999.

Nelson, Paul, "Charles Darwin on Social Darwinism," Access *Research Network,* 1996, http://www.lea-deru.com/orgs/arn/odesign/od172/1s172.htm.

New American Standard Bible Studies, "Endtime Bible Prophesy," *New American Standard Bible Studies,* 2010, http://home.flash.net/-venzor/nasbchapter2signs.htm.

Newman, Hannah, "A Report To The Jewish People About New Age Anti-Semitism," *The Rainbow Swastika,* April 15, 2001, http://searchlight.iwarp.com/articles/na_humanity.hmtl.

Nicola, Stephan, "EU Dreams Of Common Army," *Space War,* March 27, 2007, http://www.spacewar.com/reports/EU_Dreams_Of_Common_Army_999.html.

Nietzsche, Friedrich, "The Antichrist," *FNS. org*, 1895, http://www.fns.org.uk/ac.htm.

Obama, Barack, *Audacity of Hope*, New York, Crown Publishing, 2006.

Office of Strategic Services, "Hitler As He Believes Himself To Be," *The Nizkor Project*, 1991–2009, http://www.nizcor.org/hweb/people/h/hitler-adolf/oss-papers/text/oss-profile-01.html.

Office of Strategic Services, "Hitler As The German People Know Him," *The Nizkor* Project, 1991–2009, http://www.nizcor.org/hweb/people/h/hitler-adolf/oss-papers/text/oss-profile-02.html.

Office of Strategic Services, "Hitler As His Associates Know Him, Part I," *The Nizkor Project* 1991–2009, http://www.ess.uwe.ac.ul/documents/osssection3pt1.htm.

Office of Strategic Services, "Hitler As His Associates Know Him, Part II", *The Nizkor* Project, 1991–2009, http://www.ess.uwe.ac.uk/documents/osssection3pt2.htm.

Office of Strategic Services, "Report To The Bavarian State Ministry Of The Interior, Munich, 1924," *The Nizkor Project*, 1991–2009, http://www.nizcor.org/hweb/people/h/hitler-adolph/oss-papers/text/oss-sb-bavarianstaatspoli. . . .

Office of Strategic Services, "Hitler's Probable Behavior In The Future," *The Nizkor Project*, 1991–2001, http://nizcor.org/hweb/people/h/hitler-adolf/oss-papers/text/oss-profile-.06.html.

Office of Strategic Services, "Hitler Psychological Analysis & Reconstruction, Part I," *The Nizkor Project,* 1991–2009, http://www.ess.uwe.ac.uk/documents/osssection5pt1.htm.

Office of Strategic Services, "Hitler Psychological Analysis and Reconstruction, Part II," *The Nizkor Project,*1991–2009,http://www.ess.uwe.ac.uk/documents/osssection5pt2.htm.

Office of Strategic Services, "Hitler As He Knows Himself, Part I," *The Nizkor Project,* 1991–2009, http://www.ess.uwe.ac.uk/documents/osssection4pt1.htm.

Palestine Facts, "British Mandate, Grand Mufti," *Palestine Facts, Inc.,* 2010, http://www.palestine-facts.org/pf_mandate_grand_mufti.php.

Pastore, Frank, "Questions that Bother Oprah and Today's New Age Thinkers", *Townhall.com,* March 31, 2008, http://townhall.com/Common/PrintPage.aspx?f42dc2e6–69d8–4762-babo–06322a1115 . . .

Pointer, Steven R., "American Postmillennialism: Seeing the Glory," *Christian History,* January 1, 1999, http://www.christianitytoday.com/ch/61h/h.html.

Political Groove.com, "The Spiritual Foundation of the United Nations," *Political Groove.com,* 2003, http://www.politicalgroove.com/showthread.php?18865-The-Spiritual-Foundation-of-the-U—

"Quotes of Alice Bailey," *ihug.co.nz,* 1922–1960, http://homepages.ihug.co.nz/~newlight/roc/quotes.htm. (Taken from the various books by Bailey including *The Reappearance of Christ* and *A Treatise On Cosmic Fire* and five others as detailed on the website.)

Radio Free Europe, "Is Germany Closing The Door On Further EU Enlargement?," *Radio Free Europe,* March 15, 2010, http://www.rferl.org/Germany—EU_Enlargement_/1563457.html.

Rapture Christ.com, "The Rapture," *Rapture Christ.com,* April 1, 2010, http://www-rapturechrist.com/rapture2.htm.

Rapture Christ.com, "Time for the Rescue," *Rapture Christ.com* ,April 1, 2010, http://www.rapturechrist.com/time_for_the_rescue.htm

Rapture Christ.com, "Timeline for Revelation," *Rapture Christ.com,* April 1,2010, http://www.rapturechrist.com/timeline.htm.

Rast, Jennifer, "Like a Thief in the Night-The Rapture of God's Church," *Contender Ministries* , 2010, http://contenderministries.org/prophesy/rapture/trib.php.

Rast, Jennifer, "Muslim, Jewish, and Christian End-Times Prophesy Comparison," *Contender Ministries,* 2010,http://www.contenderministries.org/prophesy/eschatology.php.

Rast, Jennifer, "Prophetic Signs That We Are In The End Times," *Contender Ministries,* 2010, http://contenderministries.org/prophesy/endtimes.php.

Rawlings, Maurices S., "To Hell And Back," *Amazon.com,* 2010, http://www.emjc3.com/helland.htm.

Reagan, David, *The Master Plan,* Eugene, OR: Harvest House Publishers, 1993.

Reich, William, *The Mass Psychology of Fascism,* New York, NY: Farrar, Straus and Giroux, 2000.

Religious Counterfeits, "New Age Movement," *Religious Counterfeits*, 2000, http://www.religiouscounterfeits.org/eig.htm.

Religious Tolerance.org, "New Age Spirituality," *Religious Tolerance.org*, October 1, 2006, http://www. religious tolerance.org/newage.htm

Rickman, Gregg, "Contemporary Global Anti-Semitism—", *U.S. Department of State*, March 13, 2008, http://www.state.gov/g/drl/rls/102406.htm.

Rife, Susan B. , "War of Ideas Explores Ideology of Jihadism," Sarasota Herald Tribune, November 11, 2007, Page 11E.

Robertson, Pat, *The New World Order*, Dallas: Word Publishing, 1991.

Robinson, B. A. , "New Age Spirituality," *Religious Tolerance,org*, 2006, http://www.religious tolerance.org/newage.html.

Robinson, Meredith, "Holocaust: Eugenics, Social Darwinism and Extermination," *bhs*,2003,http://bhs.cusd220.1ake.k12.il.us/media_folder/library/Strom%20PowerPoint/Presentation1 ...

Rockefeller, David, *Memoirs*, New York: Random House, 2002.

Rocky Mountain Family Council.org, "Social Darwinism", *Rocky Mountain Family Council*, 2010, http://www.rmfc.org/fs/fs0068.html.

Rosenthal, John, "German Neo-Nazis View Islamists as Allies", *American Congress for Truth.com* , 2010, http://blog.americancongressfortruth.com/2008/10/15/german-neo-nazis-view-islamists-a—

Sarasota Herald Tribune, "Raids Target Music Promoting Hatred," *Sarasota Herald Tribune*, March 5, 2009, page 8A.

SBC.Net, "Resolution On Outcome-Based Education," *SBC.net*, June 1994, http://www.sbc.net/resolutions/resprintfriendly.asp?ID=477.

Schreiber, Bernhard, "The Men Behind Hitler," *Toolan.com*, 2003, http://www.toolan.com/hitler/index.html.

Scientific Method.com, "— A Universal Method for All Domains," *Scientific Method.com*,1992, http://www.scientific method.com/p_universal.html.

Setzer, Louis, "North Carolina Governor's School Experience," *RebirthofReason.com* ,2010, http://www.rebirthofreason.com.

Shelley, Bruce, "American Adventism: The Great Disappointment," *Christian History*, 2010, http://www.christianitytoday.com/ch/61h/61h031.html.

Smith, Warren, "Oprah and Eckhart Do the New Age Shift," *Crossroad to*, March 27, 2008, http://www.crossroad.to/articles2/08/discernment/3–27-oprah-eckhart.htm.

Spartacus, "Charlie Chaplin," *Spartacus*, 2010, http://www.spartacus.schoolnet.co.uk/USAchaplinC.htm.

Spiegel Online International, "Germany Alarmed at Far-Right Gains in East," *Spiegel Online International*, September 18, 2006, http://www.spiegal.de/international/germany/0,1518,437593,00.html.

Stewarton Bible School, Scotland, "The False Prophet," *Bible Prophesy*, December 1999, http://atschool.edu-web.co.uk/sbs777/prophesy/falsepro.html.

Stokes, William, "A Biography of Adolf Hitler," *stokesey.demon. co.uk*, 2001, http://www.stokesey.demon.co.uk/wwii/ahiltler.html.

Stoner, Peter,, "Mathematical Probability the Jesus is the Christ," *Bible Believers.org*, 2003, http://www.biblebelievers.org,au.

Sutphen, Dick, "Infiltrating the New Age Into Society," *New Age Activist,",* Summer 1986, http://www.searchlight.iwarp.com/articles/na_humanity.html.

Suster, Gerald, *Hitler: Black Magician*, London: Skoob Books Publishing Ltd.,1996.

The August Review, "Barry Goldwater Quote," (by Barry Goldwater from his book *With No Apologies*, 2079,) *The August Review*, 2010, http://www.augustreview.com/issues/globalization/the_trilateral_commission%3a_usurping_sovereignty_2007.

The History Place, "Hitler's Boyhood," *The History Place*, 1996, http://www.historyplace.com/worldwar2/riseofhitler/boyhood.htm.

The History Place, "The Rise of Hitler: Nazi Party is Formed," *The History Place*, 1996, http://www.historyplace/worldwar2/rise of hitler/party.htm.

The History Place, "Holocaust Timeline," *The History Place*, 1997, http://www.historyplace.com/worldwar2/holocaust/timeline.html

The New York Times, "Bavarian Conservative Stranglehold Feared", *The Palm Beach Post*, September 21, 2003, Page 13A.

The Wall Street Journal, "As Religious Strife Grows, Atheists Seize Pulpit, *The Sarasota Herald Tribune,* April 13, 2007, Page 7A.

Theil, Stefan, "No Country is More 'Green By Design'," *Newsweek Magazine,* July 7–14, 2008.

Tolle, Eckhart, *The Power of Now: A Guide to Spiritual Enlightenment,* Novato, CA: New World Library, 1999.

U.S. Holocaust Memorial Museum, "Antisemetism; A Continuing Threat," *U.S. Holocaust Memorial Museum,* 2008, http://www.ushmm.org/museum/exhibit/focus/antisemetism.

VeriChip Corp. com, "VeriChip Infant Protection Now Used in One-In-Three U.S. Hospitals and Birthing Centers", *VeriChip Corp.com,* December 13, 2006, http://www.verichipcorp.com/news/1166030929.

VeriMed, "Providing your personal medical information during a medical emergency," *Verimed,* 2007, http://www.verimedinfo.com/for_patients.asp.

Watchman Fellowship, Inc., "The Gospel According to Oprah," *Watchman Fellowship, Inc.,* July 1998, http://www.wfial.org/index.cfm?fuseaction=artNewAge.article_1.

Webster's New World College Dictionary, Cleveland: Wiley Publishing, Inc., 2009.

Weikart, Richard, "The Dehumanizing Impact Of Modern Thought: Darwin, Marx, Nietzsche, And Their Followers", *Discovery Institute,* July 18, 2008, http://www.discovery.org/a/6301.

Weise, Bill, 23 *Minutes in Hell,* Lake Mary, Fl: Charisma House, 2006.

Wikipedia, "Anderla, Georges," *Wikipedia*, June 5, 2009, http://en.wikipedia.org/wiki/Georges_Anderla.

Wikipedia, "Ancient Greek," *Wikipedia*, April 12, 2010, http://en.wikipedia.org/wiki/Ancient Greek.

Wikipedia, "Ayran race," *Wikipedia*, April 14, 2010, http://en.wikipedia.org/wiki/Aryan_race.

Wikipedia, "Holy Roman Empire", *Wikipedia*, April 12, 2010, http://www.wikipedia.org/wiki/Holy_Roman_Empire.

Wikipedia, "Information Age", *Wikipedia*, April 1, 2010, http://en.wikipedia.org/wiki/Information_Age.

Wikipedia, "Lucis Trust", *Wikipedia*, April 6, 2010, http://en.wikipedia.org/wiki/Lucis_Trust.

Wikipedia, "New World Order", *Wikipedia*, April 13, 2010, http://en.wikipedia.org/wiki/New_World_Order_%28conspiracy%29.

Wikipedia, "North American Free Trade Agreement", *Wikipedia*, April 13, 2010, http://en.wikipedia.org/wiki/North_American_Free_Trade_Agreement.

Wikipedia, "Theosophy", *Wikipedia*, April 9, 2010, http://en.wikipedia.org/wiki/Theosophy

Wikipedia, "United Nations", *Wikipedia*, April 3, 2010, http://wikipedia.org/wiki/United_Nations.

Will, George, "The left's anti-Semitic chic", Washington Post, (As reprinted in the *Sarasota Herald Tribune* on February 26, 2004, Page 19A.)

Wilson, Robert Anton, "Four Trends That Give Me Hope", *rawilsonfans.com*, 2003, http://www.rawilsonfans.com/articles/hope.htm.

Winfield, Nicole, "Vatican weighs in on feng shui, yoga," *The Miami Herald .com*, February 4, 2003, http://www.miami.com/mld/miamiherald/news/world/5099060.htm.

Wise Russ, "Education and New Age Humanism", *Probe Ministries*, January 14, 2002, http://www.probe.org/docs/newageed.html.

Wistrich, Robert S., "Adolf Hitler (1889–1945)", *us-israel*.org, 2003, http://www.us-israel.*org*/jsource/Holocaust/hitler.html. (Source: Wistrich, Robert S., *Who's Who in Nazi Germany*, Routledge, 1997).

Wood, Patrick, "Obama: Trilateral Commission Endgame", *The August Review*, January 30, 2009, http://www.august review.com/news_commentary/trilateral_commission/obama_trilateral_—

World Future Fund, "Internet Censorship in Germany—," *World Future Fund*, 2003, http://worldfuturefund.org/wff-master/Reading/Censor%202005/germany.Eucensor.htm.

Yahya, Harun, "Racism and Social Darwinism", *islam-denouncesantisemitism.com*,2000, http://www.islam-denouncesantisemitism.com/thesocial.htm.

Yerbury, Ray W., *Vital Signs of Christ's Return*, Green Forest, AR: New Leaf Press, 1995.

Young, Dave, "Colorado cops get first ID eye-scanners", *Fox News KDVR.com*, February 5, 2010, http://www.kdvr.com/news/kdvr-eye-identification-020510,0,6805370.story.